AT THIS
TIME OF
POTENTIAL

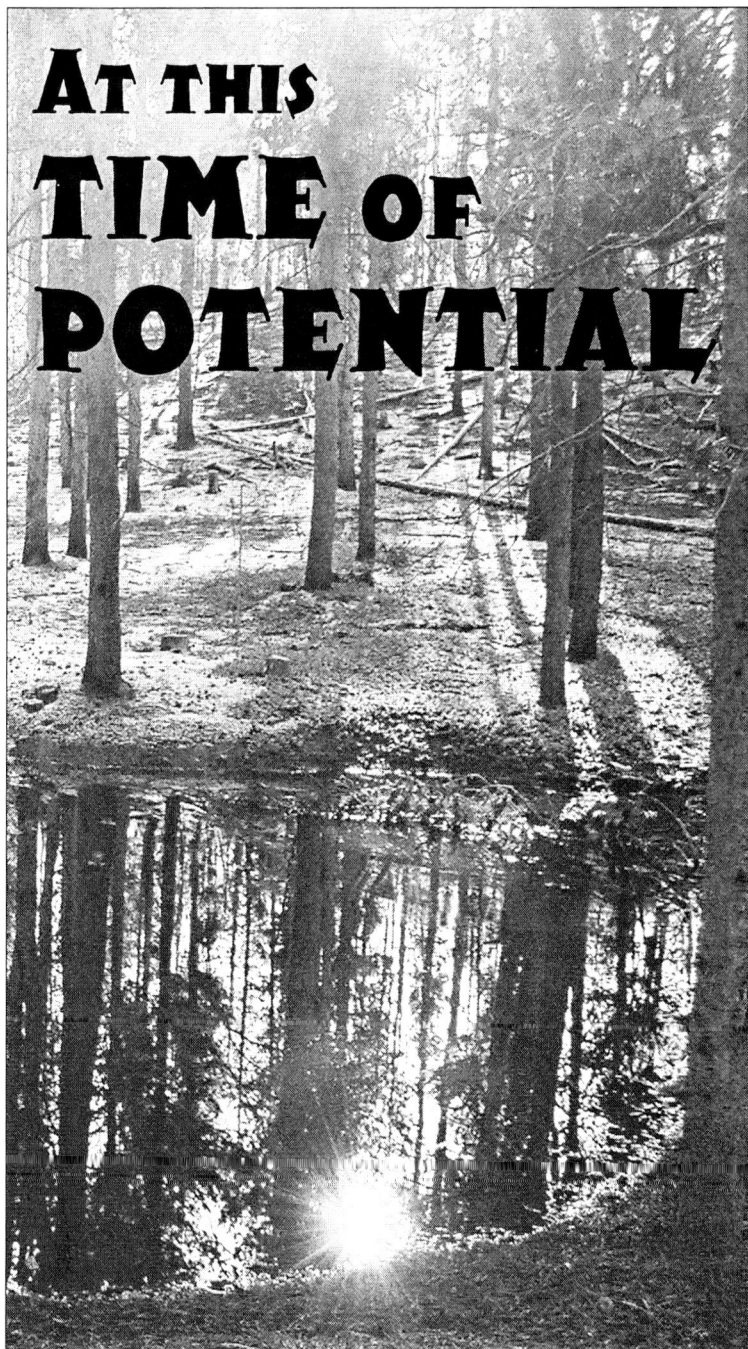

From
Path of Potential

The Desert Series Books:

Gifts of the Spirit; *Experiencing Death and Loss from the Perspective of Potential*

Becoming; *Right for the Heart... Good for the Whole (a story of repotentializing community)*

Who will Speak for Earth? *Reflections on Securing Energy from a Life of the Whole Perspective*

Developing Planetary Ethics; *the Urgent Work of Today's Generation*

Work for All Children

At this Time of Potential

The Path of Potential Library:
www.pathofpotential.org

To order books, call:

Melody Fraser
The Mail Suite
1-800-818-6177
1-970-241-8973

AT THIS
TIME OF
POTENTIAL

TERRY P. ANDERSON,
SANDRA MASLOW SMITH

Path of
Potential
TM

AT THIS TIME OF POTENTIAL

PHOTOGRAPHY
Becky Clark
BJ Clark
Bill Clark
Candi Clark
Steve Novotny
Cheryl Owens
Sandra Maslow Smith
Wes Smith
Bruce Waddell
Kathy Waddell

COVER, BOOK DESIGN, and GRAPHICS
Candi Clark

PRINTING
Precision Printing
Grand Junction, CO 81501 • www.ppgj.com

STYLISTIC EDITING
Paige Gengenbach

PUBLISHER
Path of Potential
P.O. Box 4058 • Grand Junction, CO 81502 USA
www.pathofpotential.org

AUTHORS
Terry P. Anderson
Sandra Maslow Smith

First printing – 2009
Printed in the United States of America
SFI® Certified (Sustainable Forestry Initiative) Acid Free

ABBREVIATIONS
Cf. conforms with
Ref. refer to

Path of
Potential *is a trademark of TS Potential, LLC*

ISBN-10: 0-9760139-6-7
ISBN-13: 978-0-9760139-6-9

Men and women have at their disposal an array of resources for generating greater knowledge of truth so that their lives may be ever more human. Among these is *philosophy*, which is directly concerned with asking the question of life's meaning and sketching an answer to it. *Philosophy* emerges, then, as one of the noblest of human tasks...

...With its enduring appeal to the search for truth, *philosophy* has the great responsibility of forming thought and culture, and now it must strive resolutely to recover its original vocation...

...Let *philosophers* and all *teachers of philosophy* always strive for truth, alert to the good which truth contains. Then they will be able to formulate the genuine ethics which humanity needs so urgently at this particular time.

Pope John Paul II[1]

Contents:

This time of potential...

This time of potential, this time of now, is a time that more and more of us are experiencing as...
> A time for moving towards wholeness - away from that which divides...
> A time for working for all children – all children on this earth...
> A time for advancing our humanness – for becoming fully and truly human...
> A time for grounding ourselves in intent – in intentionality.

Now, this time of potential, we see in our heart of hearts, is truly a time of synthesis...
> Synthesis of our longing to return, our yearning to become, and the truth of our being living human beings, members of the community of life...
> Synthesis requiring love to be present in the process... for *through love all things are possible (Cf. Mt 19:26; I Jn 4:8).*

Making Visible
Intended Ways of Working

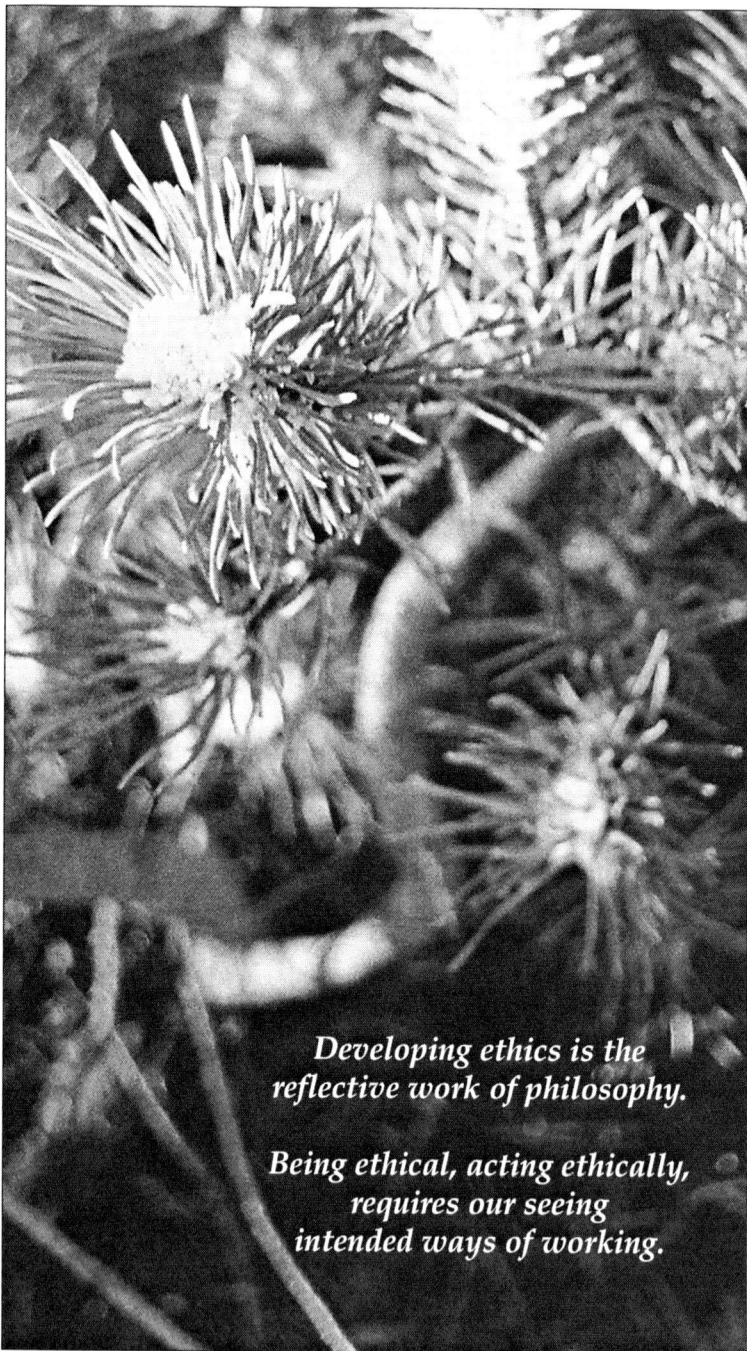

Developing ethics is the
reflective work of philosophy.

Being ethical, acting ethically,
requires our seeing
intended ways of working.

4

Completing the Desert Series

With the publishing of *At this Time of Potential*, we are experiencing a sense of completion of the writings relevant to what in our mind has become the *Desert Series*. There lies within us a sense of completing a cycle, of having come to a point of wholeness – wholeness of thought... a sense of completeness and wholeness that comes as a bit of surprise, given the unfolding nature of these *Desert Series* writings. From the very beginning, we experienced the emerging of writing in regard to the next book before the "current" book was complete. What emerged during the writing of *At this Time of Potential* was, however, quite different: a real sense of completion of writing, and a growing sense of shift in our role and work... a shift perhaps not yet clearly seen, but one that seems to be emerging as one of teaching, discussing and dialoguing.

...All of which has worked to generate some reflections on this path of writing, and some essential imagery to the particular books that "showed up" along the way... reflections not so much guided by chronological sequence, but rather some essential understandings that have a geological uniqueness to the landscape of the whole of the thought brought to light by the *Desert Series*.

In the book, *Gifts of the Spirit*,[2] we came to realize the truth of a spirit manifested being present forever, woven into the processes of life, and available to all... a truth that lifted up an essential aspect of our work on earth, our way of joining in and contributing to the unfolding creation... an understanding further deepened by the reflection of a wise elder who shared with us the truth of her life experience: *Until you lose your fear of death, you cannot truly experience life.*

5

Then there are the earth books: *Who will Speak for Earth?*[3] and *Developing Planetary Ethics.*[4] The common pattern of our writing is to sustain a reflective process – a reflective state of mind – and then strive to capture with words, very specific words, the image that the reflective process gives to us.

With the earth books, the necessity for holding a life of the whole perspective became absolutely clear. Seeing ourselves as part of life - intentionally, not accidently, a part of life – brought to the fore a unique, much richer, deeper and more authentic approach to our living on earth with intended harmony. We came to see that unless we understand the intended way of working – the intended way of working of earth, of life, of life processes, of life itself – we cannot, in reality, be ethical... we cannot live from, or go forward in ways that are authentically ethical... all of which lift up the necessity for developing understanding of such things as purpose, intended ways of working, etc., a truth relevant to the whole of creation, but one seemingly equally relevant to the structures, processes and systems that we as living human beings create.

The book, *Becoming,*[5] is the ongoing story of the people of Kennett Square, the story of their work to live from a philosophy, a living philosophy emerging from the virtue – the essence, the intended essential way of working - of the land... an ongoing effort that continues to illuminate the coalescing power – the power to build and become community - through the sharing of a common philosophy that emerges from the essence of the land itself... a process that not only reflects our inherent capacity as living beings to tune into and to be tuned by the intended working of the land, but also our ableness to transcend that which normally causes separation, division, etc.

6

The book, *Work for All Children*,[6] is in some ways a bringing together in one book, of the essential tenets of the living philosophy of potential... a book sourced in an image, or perhaps more accurately a charcoal sketch, of the living philosophy of potential, with a particular emphasis on the children – all the children, the children of earth. We saw within the writing, and within the title itself, the necessity and power within the question: *Will this – which we are about to create, to pursue, to do – work for all children?* We also saw that regardless of where we are in life, we can take up a role in regards to working for all children. Thus we could see the relevant guidance of "work for all children" not only in terms of ourselves as individuals, but as a community, as a country... as a people of earth.

This last book that completes the cycle, the book, *At this Time of Potential*, was in many ways, to us, the most surprising of all. Recalling that these *Desert Series* books are not pre-planned by us, but rather just emerge through an unfolding process, we were a bit surprised and somewhat taken back as these particular writings began to "show up"... writings that included reflections from a life of the whole perspective on some of the Gospels... Gospels that we began to think of as the "going forward" Gospels... surprising in that our work for many years, in some ways our lifelong work, had been the imaging and articulation of a living philosophy of potential... a philosophy that we saw as complementary to the "faith/salvation/longing to return" aspect of ourselves, but one that was clearly distinct from religions, theology, etc. For this reason, the Gospels – our own personal lifelong source of the word - seemed to be outside of the territory of the living philosophy of potential. However this time of potential is *a time of moving*

7

towards wholeness, away from that which divides, a wholeness that requires within us as a people a synthesis of the word and the works – the word and the works being the manifestation of the intent of the Source of creation. The reflective writings that have emerged from the perspective of potential seem to have brought forth some imagery and understandings helpful, and perhaps essential, to the process and our work towards becoming – fulfilling the intent of our Creator, of becoming fully and truly human. This book, as is true of all the books and writings of the *Desert Series*, is aimed at enabling a process, the process of an upward shift and advancement in our humanness... an evolutionary step in becoming fully and truly human... a process with which we are being called to cooperate... a process that reflects the intentionality of the Common Source of all life, of all people on earth – the Source of the whole of creation.

Finally, what we have come to see and understand is that the philosophy of potential, as articulated in the *Desert Series*, is sufficiently whole and complete to provide fertile ground for revitalizing America's philosophy.

Synthesis for Wholeness

The aim of the living philosophy of potential is to enable our "moving towards wholeness, away from that which divides"... movement increasingly recognized as being absolutely necessary. Critical to our ableness to move towards wholeness is our developing an understanding of essence, and the developing of our capacity for the compassion of caring about – the compassion of equality, of each of us at essence being equal. It is through essence and the compassion of caring about that synthesis – synthesis for wholeness – becomes possible.

Enabling this aim is the working purpose of the living philosophy of potential:

...Making visible the path of our potential by taking things to essence from the life of the whole perspective...

...in a way that we can see and understand the intention and intended ways of working...

...such that the synthesis for wholeness – the wholeness of intent – can be brought about through intuitive, reflective processing.

In particular at this time of potential, a time of great faith - a time to be more intentional about our purposes, more holistic in our approaches - we find that both the word and the works are the "things" to be taken to essence from the life of the whole perspective... always remembering that community is the smallest whole within which intention can be unfolded - communities organized around particular work, intentional purposes, and life of the whole aims.

9

In previously published *Desert Series* books, particularly in *Work for All Children*, the essence of the works from the life of the whole perspective has been addressed. In this book, *At This Time of Potential*, we are beginning to address taking the word to essence from the life of the whole perspective. It is the hope that through reflection and reflective dialogue on these beginnings, each and all will see more clearly their called work in the community on the path of moving towards intended wholeness – towards the wholeness of humanity in working to harmonize with the intentional life processes of the ongoing unfolding creation.

In
the context of our country and
of our working for all children in the
world, the work of the living philosophy
of potential is making visible
the path of potential – the path of
intentionality.

Unfolding Potential

In keeping with the working purpose of the living philosophy of potential, over the past many years, our work has been and is making visible the path of potential... *potential being the intentionality of the Creator enfolded within the spirit of each and all as our unique essence.* As living human beings, joining with the process – harmonizing with and enabling the process – of unfolding the potential enfolded within, is at the heart and core of our work and role on this earth.

Potential emanates from – is a direct reflection of – the intention of the Creator. We have confidence in our being on the path of our Creator's intention when we can see the rightness and goodness in the direction we are pursuing and the actions we are taking... right for the one, good for the whole. And we have authentic hope - we can be truly hopeful - when the changes we seek represent real advances in our humanness, advances which move us towards becoming fully and truly human, as intended.

Intention – our Creator's intentionality – preceded, came before, both the word and the works. It is through the seeing of the truth in the manifested word and works of the Creator that we gain access to a deeper understanding of intention. Philosophy, in particular the living philosophy of potential, holds as its primary focus the intentional works and intended ways of working of life on earth, the whole of life of which we as living human beings are a part, and within which we have a significant role to play – a true calling. The seeing of truth, of gaining a deeper sense of intention and intended ways of working, requires reflection and calls upon the intuition of wholeness - the wholeness called for at this time of potential, a time for moving towards wholeness and away from that which divides.

It is through the work of unfolding potential that spirit is manifested, spirit that becomes woven into the processes of life itself. Reflection and reflective dialogue are essential to the unfolding of potential... unfolding potential being sharply different from our common experience of problem-solving or pursuing what is possible in the absence of potential and wholeness, or of rightness and goodness. Some helpful questions for guiding and assessing our efforts in regards to unfolding potential:

• <u>Am I working from an image of creating what could be?</u>

• <u>Is the means by which I am reaching this image one of reaction or reflection?</u> Reflection is the process through which we are given the gift of seeing potential – seeing the essence of each within the ongoing life of the whole.

• <u>Will this change not only be right for each, but good for all? Is it good for all children of earth and right for the whole of the larger community?</u> True change – change that makes a difference, change in harmony with the intended unfolding – works for all children and elevates the community, moving it towards wholeness.

• <u>Is love flowing through my heart as I work to bring forth the potential enfolded within?</u> The essence of the Creator's intention is love, and love is the Creator's process. We know, in our heart of hearts, that... *if love is not present in the process, love will not be present in the outcome.*

Love in the Process

Early on in our work along the path of potential, even before the emergence of the living philosophy of potential, the intuitively knowable truth, "if love is not present in the process, love will not be present in the outcome," became an anchor point, and a true source of discernment for that which was pursued or joined with. This truth, along with the understanding of there being intent, and intended ways of working (the process perspective of design), became both cornerstone and keystone for the work of the living philosophy of potential. Given this cornerstone of love, it is not surprising that when the time came for us to reflect from the perspective of the living philosophy of potential on the manifested intent we commonly think of as the word, we would turn, for the most part, to the Gospel teachings of Christ... Christ being regarded as an exemplar in matters of love, and peace as well, even by many of those who have no religious or belief system orientation towards his teaching. We also recognized that it was not the work of the living philosophy of potential – at least through the authors' reflection and writing – to deal with the totality of the revealed word. That work, we expect, will take place through ongoing reflection and reflective dialoguing within community. The particular Gospel teachings that we were drawn to are those that we have come to think of as the "going forward" teachings, the teachings we were intended to strive to live and work from in a going forward way after Christ returned to the Father, teachings that themselves are anchored in the two Commandments:

"Love God" and
"Love one another as I have loved you" (Cf. Mt 22:37; Jn 13:34).

Both of these Commandments have significance to the cornerstone of the living philosophy of potential, "if love is not present in the process, love will not be present in the outcome."

Now, while we lack the life experience to be authentic in regards to the interpretations of the revealed word brought forth by the world's religions, we do have an experience, a commonly shared experience, that is for many of us a true source of hope. Our experience is that when people come together with a shared aim of advancing our humanness, an aim bolstered by a conviction of this being the necessary work of our time – this time of potential, this time of moving towards wholeness and away from that which divides - that which was previously thought of as impossible, becomes possible... or more accurately, what emerges through reflective dialogue is beyond what we had imagined or hoped for. In this work, religion – the various religious faiths of those involved in the dialogues - rather than being a cause of separation, is both an enriching source... and that which is enriched through reflective dialoguing where love is present in the process.

Throughout history there have been expressions of wisdom and understanding in regards to the complementary working of faith and philosophy, of religion and science, etc. Pope John Paul II and Albert Einstein, for example, were quite clear in their reflections on this complementarity. One notion that seems to have particular relevance at this time is that faith without philosophy risks becoming a myth.[7,8] Without doubt, reflection and reflective dialoguing on this wisdom would yield much seeing in regards to this essential complementarity, a seeing beyond the scope of this writing. We can, however, if we hold in mind the critical issues (peace, ecology, poverty, for example) facing humankind and all of life on earth, see the usefulness of a philosophy that is intentional in its orientation, and whole enough such that we can come together to move towards wholeness and away from that which divides... a living philosophy, a practiceable philosophy that, given its cornerstone of love in the process, can be an enriching source of reflection, as well as an enabler of oneness, wholeness and completeness to those whose faith is anchored in love emanating from a single Source. And too, experience shows the living philosophy of potential can be an equally enriching and inspiriting source of reflection for those who are not drawn to organized faith, but are drawn towards advancing our humanness, our moving towards wholeness, those whose efforts and intentions demand an understanding of the essence of our humanness... an understanding of compassion, in particular the compassion of equality... the nature of compassion called for at this time of potential.

The Truth of Our Oneness,
Working Towards Wholeness[9]

The sense of oneness – oneness as a people, oneness with the universe – comes about quite readily through reflection and contemplation. The truth of our oneness – one people, one earth – is not only clear through reflecting on the works of the Creator, but equally clear through the teachings of Christ – particularly through his words as he responded to the request to teach us to pray: *"Our Father"* (Mt 6:9)... our Common Father, of whom we are all children, children of the one and the same God. Yet, as we well know, the acceptance of this truth – of living it out – still provides for us a bit of a struggle.

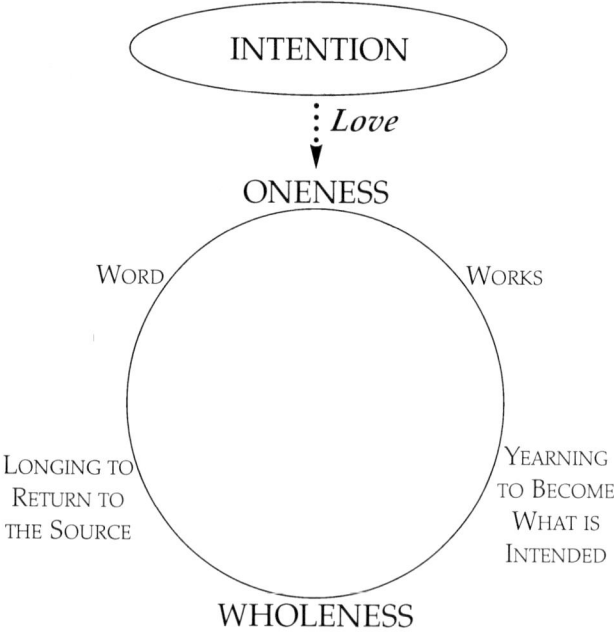

INTENTION

Love

ONENESS

WORD   WORKS

LONGING TO RETURN TO THE SOURCE

YEARNING TO BECOME WHAT IS INTENDED

WHOLENESS

Wholeness, on the other hand, takes greater effort to gain some clarity of... which is strange in a way, because for many of us, the notion of wholeness is a source of discord in our lives. This discord, at essence, has as its source, two urges – our longing to return to the Ultimate Source, and our yearning to become. This becoming – the discovery of purpose, our reason for being, our work, our calling – has been present as an urge within us, but not really address-able because of the absence of philosophy – the absence of a practical, practice-able, living philosophy; a void that, if it continues to exist, not only has severe consequences to us personally, but one that hinders, if not halts our ability to advance our humanness.

If oneness and wholeness, two truths of our existence, truths of the intent and intended ways of working of our Creator, are to become real for us, a synthesis of the path to salvation (the path of returning to the Source) and the path of potential (the path of our becoming fully and truly human) must occur. There is much hope in the willingness to go back to essence – to take issues to essence… to see essential truths, and right and good working of the whole within which issues exist, or to which issues relate. By so doing, wis-dom and wise choices become possible… and of course this way of working makes increasingly possi-ble the bringing about of a harmonious relatedness between the path to God and the path of our work on earth, the path of fulfilling the intent and intended ways of working of the Creator.

The Going Forward Gospels

There is hope, real hope in the Gospels... hope not only in relation to our longing to return – to return to the Source of our creation – but hope equally significant at this time, in regards to our yearning to become - to fulfilling our role, to becoming fully and truly human... as intended...

...Hope fully present to the seeing heart, the heart seeking wisdom, essential wisdom for the here and now, the unfolding now...

...Hope that gives access to Spirit – the Spirit being called for at this time of potential...

A time for moving towards wholeness, away from that which divides...

A time for conscious, intentional becoming, becoming fully and truly human...

A time for fulfilling our role, our intended instrumental role, in the intended unfolding of all of life on earth...

A time for love in our processes.

Much seeable truth and understanding – truth and understanding relative to our yearning to become - lies within the Gospels... seeable through reflection and reflective dialogue from a perspective of potential, a perspective that embraces the complementary notion and work of becoming – complementary to the notion of salvation, the work of returning.

The particular Gospels reflected upon in these writings are increasingly thought of as the "going forward" Gospels, the teachings of Christ that reflect intended ways for us - as we go forward on this earth, after his departure - teachings that in many ways are centered in the two Commandments, *"Love God,"* and *"Love one another as I have loved you"* (Cf. Mt 22:37; Jn 13:34), with particular emphasis on the latter, the oft called new Commandment... a perhaps not surprising emphasis given the cornerstone of the perspective of the living philosophy of potential: *If love is not present in the process, love will not be present in the outcome.*

Reflecting on the first Commandment – to love God – an image emerges, an image of a way to love God is to honor the intended way of working of life in the world... an image and perspective that is strengthened and clarified through the seeing that at essence, the original sin – the first sin of humankind - was the interfering with the intended way of the working of life in the world.

Sustaining a Reflective Process

All *Desert Series* books are about reflection. Their purpose is to engender and enable the process of reflecting, a particular reflecting aimed at awakening within that which is significant to ourselves... a significance perhaps not yet fully understood, but one that nevertheless has a seeking, questioning presence... a heartfelt presence... a truth for us that is itself in the process of unfolding... an unfolding that is halted or stymied by analysis, efforts to "figure it out," or inner arguing.

Experience has shown it is better, more fruitful, more meaningful, to read through – to continue without analytical pauses... sustaining the reflective character in one's reading by following the pattern, the cyclical process pattern, of intuition... a pattern that invites us to openly and receptively read and reread... trusting that in this way, understanding images of the significant will emerge.

The Creator is unfathomable...
The Creator's intent is knowable...
Thus "Thy Will" is possible.

Part 1

Taking up the Path of Intentionality

Perhaps the truest expression, the very essence of our being created in the image and likeness of the Creator (Cf. Gen 1:27), is our inherent ableness to be intentional...

Likewise, the greatest gift we can return to our Creator is the exercising of our free will towards becoming and being intentional...

For it is through intentionality that love enters into the working of the world...

And it is in this way that "Thy Will" will be done on this earth, at this time... this time of potential and intentional purpose.

*The seed of our potential springs to life,
is awakened from its dormancy by the
nourishing light of intentionality.*

Reflecting on Becoming Intentional

Have you ever thought about how interesting it is that in our culture, faith and philosophy are left to meet in the heart of the person? Where is the help we need to be able to hold the two together, shining the light, the light that would tell us whether the two together are leading to completeness – to becoming fully and truly human – or whether they are fragments, incongruent with one another and leading away from wholeness? Certainly, we are unaccustomed to holding the two – faith and philosophy – together and up to the same light. If we are to do so, what light would we shine on them? Ought not they come together, synthesize, at intentionality? Now whether we come from faith or living philosophy, we see intentionality comes before the beginning. From the side of faith, intentionality was before – preceded - all; from the side of living philosophy, intentionality - image and will - come before the act.

And so, intentionality is where we search if we wish to synthesize within ourselves the word and the works – synthesize within ourselves our path of returning and our path of becoming into one whole harmonious path. Intentionality is where we search if we are on the path – or seeking the path – of becoming… becoming fully and truly human, becoming that which was intended by our design, unfolding the potential enfolded within.

Where there is a need to become, we are drawn to the path of intentionality. Perhaps the closest we humans can get to the seeing of intentionality comes through reflection - reflecting on wholes and going to essence - all the time having faith that the image of what we need will be given – that the wisdom will be given when our hearts are open. If it is intent we seek to understand – understand at the level essential for our becoming – then we take things to essence from a life of the whole perspective.

At this time of potential, more and more of us are experiencing the need to synthesize - in our heart of hearts - the truths of the word and the works. To do so calls each to reflect not only on the works of creation, but also on the words of revelation... calls each to reflect on essential truths revealed through both the word and the works... to reflect on both from a life of the whole perspective, and seeking essence.

Ultimately,
the perspective we hold
determines the life path we take,
our thinking and behavior along that path,
and the way we live and work.

Shifting Our Perspective

It is not uncommon for we, the people of earth, to think about and see things as if they are separate and isolated one from another. It would seem that the fact of our physical separateness deludes us into believing we are independent of one another. Yet the truth is we are each a living element, a systemic member of one living whole – the whole of humanity… we are each a part of the living earth – intentional members of earth's life community… and we hold within us the yet to be unfolded living potential to become one with our Creator. Jesus, when speaking to the Samaritan woman at the well (Ref. Jn 4:4-42), looked to her heart. She was not separate and separable; she was not untouchable; she was a living part of a whole people, the people of earth… and he was working to bring the whole of people – the soul of humanity – to become one living intentional whole.

When we reflect on the story of the woman at the well in this way, we learn much about the progression of development - of change - required of us. One barrier to get beyond is what we have been taught by our culture, beyond teaching that separates rather than unites all people, beyond teaching that some people are clean and some unclean, that some have the power and authority to differentiate and isolate others… beyond teaching that moves us not towards truth, but away from truth.

A second essential shift in perspective is letting go of our attachment to the physical - attachment to what we gain through the senses - as being all that is real. We are called to shift from seeing only with our eyes to "seeing" with our hearts. In the physical world, we depend on water for life; in the world of the Spirit, living water – love - is the wellspring of life. With our eyes we see that our bodies and all of life itself need water to be able to live and flourish. With our hearts we "see" that our souls require living water – the love of the Creator – to be able to flourish and live in unity with one another as we serve the purpose of our existence. We need both; we thirst for both. Yet unfortunately we mostly fail to realize the second thirst – the thirst that is truly our primary, our preeminent, thirst – and search to be refreshed by things of the world that cannot nor ever will satisfy our thirst for the Creator's love. We search existence for Spirit, yet the answers we find in the existence world are vinegar when it comes to satisfying this thirst.

To the woman at the well, Jesus said, *"Go call your husband and come here"* (Jn 4:16). Humanity, symbolized by the heart of the Samaritan woman, must deal with past spouses – the different gods we have worshiped, identified with, and loved... loves unable to provide the living water we so desperately need. Presently we are all, in some way, worshiping a false god (the man with whom she was presently living would not become her spouse). We must face our life and come to grips with our false loves. The perspective shift calls for focusing our hearts and our love on the one true Source, the Father. Jesus goes on to say that worship will not be dependent upon place. The hazard of focus on place had shown itself among the Pharisees who had kept people from the Source by lording over them. Authority and position had become their spouse, their false love. They made themselves as teacher and judge, but did not understand anything about the essentiality of worshiping God in Spirit and truth. Their rules and laws were barriers to people seeing *"God is Spirit, and those worshipping him need to worship in Spirit and truth"* (Jn 4:24).

Essential is shifting our hearts... shifting to believing in what is unseen, believing in a world of Spirit and truth - a faith through which all that is necessary will be revealed such that it becomes possible that our work may do the will of the Father, thereby feeding our souls and fulfilling the purpose of our life. For we are each and all created and called to take our systemic part in the working of the whole of humanity and the whole of life on earth. Much has been accomplished before we have appeared on this earth, yet the Father's work is unfinished. To do the Father's will, *"We reap what we did not sow"* (Cf. Jn 4:37-38). This is our role; this is our work... to do the will of the Father by taking a role in finishing his work. Herein lies the essentiality of faith. We cannot "see" all; we cannot know all. Yet we will be given all that we need to do the work of the Father, and by so doing, play a part in the calling of humanity to drink the love of Christ, and wholeheartedly return to the Father the love for which our Father thirsts.

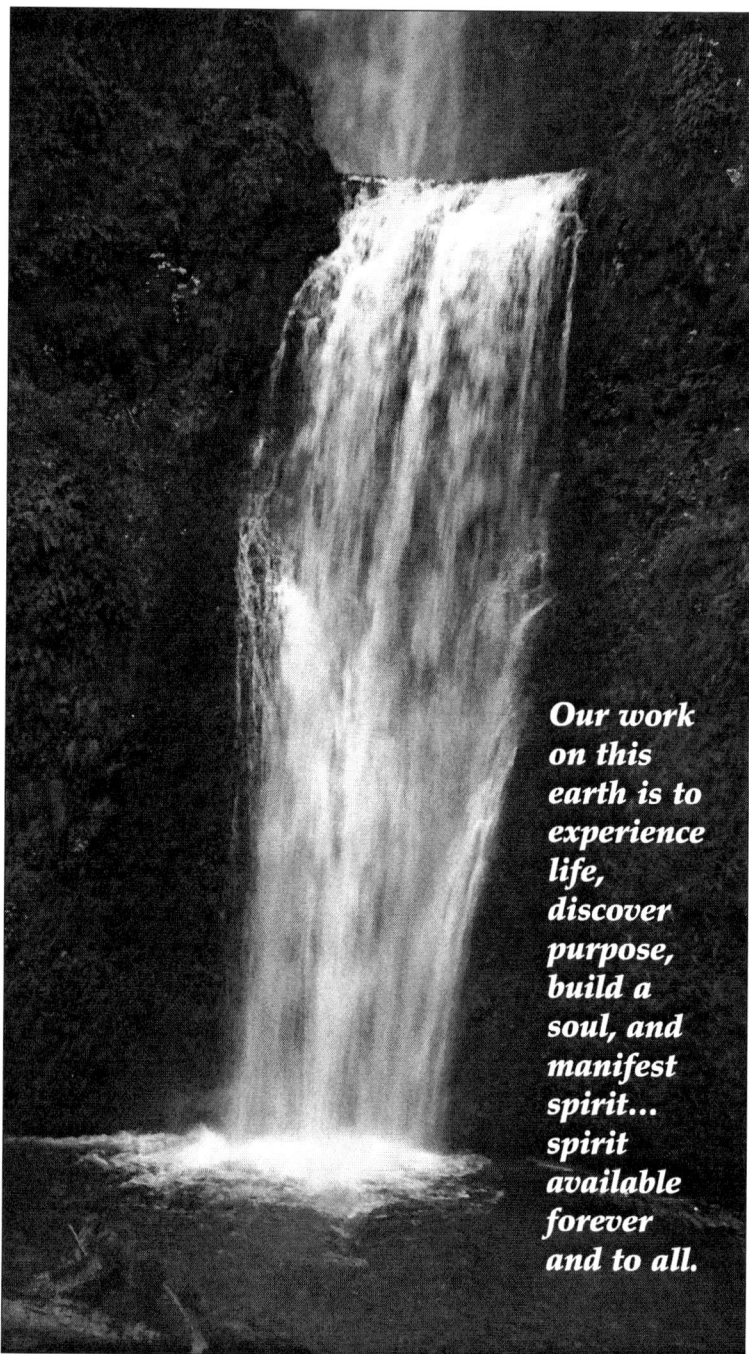

Our work on this earth is to experience life, discover purpose, build a soul, and manifest spirit... spirit available forever and to all.

Being Generated from Above

We are told, from the heart of Jesus – *"Truly, truly I say to you, if one is not generated from above, he is not able to see the kingdom of God"* (Jn 3:3). There are two worlds - the world of the sensory and the world of the Spirit. Images, visions and so-called inspirations that are generated from and by the sensory, remain sensory. The world of existence is not able to lift itself by itself to a higher plane. We are born of the flesh, and we die, going back to the earth. Equally true, we must also be generated of Spirit – from above – thus becoming able to "see" the kingdom of God... thereby able to fulfill the intention of our Creator.

Christ chides Nicodemus (Ref. Jn 3:1-21) for his lack of belief. For Christ knows that as we live on this earth, we have access to two experiences - the sensory and the spiritual: *"The Spirit breathes where he desires, and you hear his voice; but you do not know from where he comes, and where he goes; so is everyone who has been generated from the Spirit... If I told you earthly things, and you do not believe, how will you believe if I tell you heavenly things?"* (Jn 3:8, 12). If we do not believe we can hear the voice of the Spirit, then we will never believe the truths that the Spirit has given to us! In believing, we might come to "see" and "hear"... and what we "see" and what we "hear" becomes that which we manifest – the will of the Creator given through the voice of the Spirit. Manifesting the things of heaven, the will of the Creator – being generated out of Spirit – is spirit... and a spirit manifested has life everlasting – *"Thy kingdom come... on earth as in heaven"* (Mt 6:10).

The Spirit entered earth through Christ... becoming everlastingly available to humankind on earth. It is for this he came to earth... his soul returning to the Father, but the Spirit remaining here forever.

We are made in the image and likeness of the Creator. We, too, are potential instruments of the Spirit. To become instruments of the Spirit – to be generated of Spirit and to manifest spirit ourselves, spirit available forever and to all – is why we came to earth in the first place.

Going Your Way

The "woman caught in adultery" (Ref. Jn 8:1-11) learned the truth: the truth is we are all equal at essence. With this woman standing before him, a woman about to be stoned for her act of disobedience to the law, Jesus gives his attention, not directly to her, but to the would-be stoners: *"Let he among you who is without sin cast the first stone"* (Jn 8:7). Conscience becomes the judge... conscience which is directly given from the Source... conscience which focuses our attention on what we ourselves have done, are doing, have not done. And so, Jesus points the way... the way is through our hearts. Our acts must come through our hearts. When love flows into and through us, we see that we are not separate from one another; we are not hierarchical to one another; we are all part of one whole - equal parts of one living whole. What the woman caught in adultery realized was that she had sinned; yet there was hope... hope because each and all realized at the same time, their own sinfulness. This story reveals to all, the truth that God sees and knows more about us than we do. *"He searches the hearts of men"* (Cf. Rom 8:27).

And then, when it seems all is lost but life itself, hope enters: Jesus said the words, *"Neither do I condemn you"* (Jn 8:11). The focus is changed! For Jesus' way is to speak not of our physical life, our external life, but of our spiritual life. He tells her - tells us - he does not condemn her. Our spiritual life is not here lost! The Pharisees were giving all of their attention to existence – to this world: Remove her from this world; she has no right to live – she is less than us! Jesus tells her, you are not condemned in the world that truly counts – in the world of the Spirit. And then, he goes farther; he gives her the hope of and the key to sustaining the gift she has been given. *"Go, and sin no more"* (Jn 8:11)... you are a part of this living whole of life. You were intended and are designed to fill a role in life. You have a calling. Your way is to *"Take up your cross"* (Cf. Mt 10:38) and answer your calling... never again leave the path of your calling.

What is life and what is death? Death comes when we turn our backs on our hearts - on our consciences - and live and act from "my will," not "Thy Will." We are physically alive – the heart is beating – but we are really dead – closed – to the Creator's ever-flowing guiding love. "Life" is when that love flows through us, when we open ourselves to that love, manifesting it in the world in the unique way for which we are intended and designed. When the Creator's love flows into and through us, when we say "Yes" to our calling, and when we become instruments of the Creator, then *"Thy kingdom comes, and Thy will is done on earth as in heaven"* (Cf. Mt 6:10). Then there will be hope... and freedom. Jesus gave to the woman about to be stoned the gift of hope: hope to live... hope for humanity... hope for her eternal destiny... hope for a life of meaning - she has a special way, a role to fill, a calling within the whole... hope that she truly can go forth and be and become as intended.

A Seeing of Truth

I became aware of being in a vision... a holographic or three-dimensional vision. It was like being in a bubble and all were in the bubble... we all were there together.

I was standing next to this personage who had the being of Christ. All of my discernment said that Christ was who was there. We were standing there with two scenes in front of us – one to the left and one to the right. He was standing with one foot in each of these images.

It was a totally silent image. This personage and I were standing side-by-side. Words did not feel necessary. The envisioning and the experiencing of the presence began to work innerly... as expressed thoughts. His hands were out, and what was before us was obvious. I had an overwhelming sense of togetherness. Then the words became present, but not with sound. I am saying this in a sequential manner; yet it did not happen sequentially, but all at once. I am describing what was heard, seen and experienced, without interpretation.

The left-hand scene was clear imagery. It was people standing with rocks in their hands, and a woman cowering in the corner against the wall. The right-hand scene was a very fuzzy mirror image of the scene on the left. We could see the shapes and forms, but the faces were fuzzy... in a sense, I could not tell if they were being created or erased. I almost felt that if I could turn on the light, then maybe I would be able to see it more clearly. That is when the image of "becoming" showed itself in the scene on the right. The personage of Christ put his right hand over, and I then had the sense this side is "becoming," while the left-hand side is all "salvation."

Then the "becoming side" words were spoken, "If love is not present in the process, love will not be present in the outcome." The mirror image of those words on the "salvation" side were *"Let he among you who is without sin cast the first stone"* (Jn 8:7). The words of love – the words of becoming - were in the same voice – Christ's voice – and were the mirror of the words of salvation.

Stone silence... I could "see" the words. They were being written. The words in each side were on a plank... it was the conscience plank. The words were so clear... there was no confusion in the words.

While those faces and shapes of humans on the right side were fuzzy, I could see they were single persons and groups – any person or group we find ourselves personifying as the enemy in order to achieve our goals. These fuzzy people standing around all had rocks in their hands. They personified any group that you have to motivate to pick up the rock to stone the perceived enemy. There were environmentalists, politicians, rights and peace activists, government, business and religious leaders, and on and on and on. At any time, anyone could be throwing and anyone could be thrown at. This is what made "If love is not present in the process, love will not be present in the outcome" the mirror of *"Whoever is without sin, throw the first rock"* (Cf. Jn 8:7).

As his arm opened and reached out to the left, Christ said, "This is what was unfolding then," and to the right, "and this is what is unfolding now."

All of this began to be drawn into me, outerly disappearing... then innerly, these words came: "Life, liberty and the pursuit of dignity." Then came "Experience the fullness and wholeness of life... that is what America is for - a place for that." Then, "Liberty

– the freedom to choose the process by which I develop my soul, realize my potential, and surrender to my instrumentality." Then the words were, "Pursuit of dignity - become fully and truly human in the dignified image that was intended." As the bubble – all of both images and Christ – started being absorbed into me, these thoughts were unfolding... and the inner experience was that of joyous nervousness. I was experiencing the doubtless realness of what was occurring as I stood there outside the morning shower.

There was no pre-thought before the vision came. It was just there... and it coalesced all.

We look to the "going forward"
teachings of Christ for creating a
disciplined way of life...
an "intentional, every day"
- at home and at work – way of life.

42

Standing in the Stream of Becoming

Christs: *"I am the way, and the truth, and the life"* (Jn 14:6).

Essence of Christ's teaching:
   "Love God, the Father" (Cf. Mt 22:37; 6:9).
   "Love one another as I have loved you" (Jn 13:34).

Christ's work:
   Through dying, re-open the path of return - make it
      possible for humankind to return to the Source.
   Through Spirit, the manifestation of Spirit - make it
      possible for humankind to realize our potential,
      our potential to become fully and truly human,
      to fulfill the Creator's intent and intended ways
      of working.

   We too have work related to becoming – work
that is unique to us but shares the aim of advancing
humanness, and enriching life – the life of the whole
and the whole of life on this earth.
   By standing in the upward advancing stream of
evolution – the stream of becoming – we can join in the
intended unfolding... and, with discipline and receptivity - listening with our heart - we can discover and,
at the very least, stay on a path towards our intended
work, and put forth meaningful effort to carry it out.
   In order to stand in the stream of becoming, we
need to strive to come from our essence pattern – to be
true to our heart – rather than be determined and
defined by existence. Being externally defined keeps
us firmly on the bank. Nothing is so helpful for wad-
ing into the stream of becoming as purpose – intentional purpose that serves the larger whole of which
we are a part.

To be of Christ is to be of *"the way, and the truth, and the life"* (Jn 14:6).

The Way – *"Love God… love one another as I have loved you"* (Cf. Mt 22:37; Jn 13:34).

The Truth – Wisdom, the Creator's intention during the process of creation.

The Life – The whole of life, the life of the whole. Humanity, like all other members of life, can only realize its potential through purposes that serve "the larger whole." For humanity – the community of people on earth, earth's people – the larger whole is the whole of life, perhaps not surprising, given earth's purpose is to provide a place for life to enter into the working of the universe – the unfolding creation. Thus purpose – intentional purpose – finds the whole of life as "the whole" which it serves.

Only Life can re-inspirit the intended unfolding path of life itself.

Keeping the Commandments

Christ, as he prepared to ascend to the Father, clearly – in his heart and his mind – was not abandoning us, but rather putting in place all that which would be needed by us for going forth... going forth along the way, the path that he had opened up for us... for us to advance in our humanness... to be and become fully and truly human... fully and truly human in the manner of Christ, and in the image intended by our Creator.

Love, the essence of the Father, was intended to be the core, the very heart of, the essence of the way, of the path, of the going forward process of advancing our humanness. Thus the two Commandments, one being familiar and old: *"Love God"* (Mt 22:37), which through Christ became a spiritual synthesis of all previous Commandments, all of which were particular manifestations of the spiritual essence of the Father... love itself, and its only Source.

The second Commandment, the new one – *"Love one another as I have loved you"* (Jn 13:34) - experienced by those who knew or come to know Jesus, and as yet neither fully understood, nor truly lived out, was intended to be the means by which we become disciples, true disciples of Christ... true followers of *"the way, and the truth, and the life"* (Jn 14:6)... followers imbued, embedded, with love – as instruments for love entering into the process of intended unfolding... instruments, saying "Yes," in the manner of Mary and Christ (Ref. Lk 1:38, Ref. Mt 26:39), to our instrumentality such that the will of the Father can freely enter into the working of the world... this world, our world, this earth upon which "Thy Will," the will of the Father, is intended to be done.

It is through the Spirit, the Spirit of truth, entering into receptive hearts that it becomes possible for us to live out – to experience in life – the two Commandments: *"To love* (truly love) *God,"* and to *"love one another as I have loved you"* (Cf. Mt 22:37; Jn 13:34)... and by so doing, to love Christ... to love Christ by keeping his Commandments. To follow the Commandments of Christ requires much inner processing of the heart; an inner processing enabled by reflection and dialogue of the nature required to be open to the Spirit, to gain access to wisdom, and to develop the capacity to see and understand intended working.

Realizing our Potential

Love in the process is what we innerly experience within our own self as well as between and among ourselves when we are truly working – operating – in sync with intended ways of working; while working in ways that enable the unfolding of ever present potential... the unfolding of potential, be it within the living nature of a material, a particular situation, or life itself – its members, its processes, its systems...

Love being present in the process is the means by which we advance our humanness... a presence made real through the honoring of essence, our moving towards wholeness, and the enabling of the realization of potential... in particular, our potential to become fully and truly human as intended.

Keeping Open the Pathway of Love

Christ was clear – particularly in his dying words on the cross, *"Father forgive them, they know not what they are doing"* (Lk 23:34) - that only the Father could forgive. What then is the teaching in his prayer when he lifts up the notion *"...as we forgive those who trespass against us"* (Cf. Mt 6:12)?

Forgiveness is a particular manifestation of love – the love of our Creator, a love that transcends all acts – even the crucifixion of his Son. We are not the source of love, but are so designed that love can enter into and through us. Thus we can pray to the Father for forgiveness. We can turn and open our hearts to his forgiving love, an unceasing love that is never denied, always willing to flow into a receptive heart - a receptive heart, and a heart that can choose. We are so designed that we can choose love as our start point... or we can choose anger and hate. Thus we have the potential to not only choose, but also forgive.

It is the way of life to be trespassed. The heart that turns away from anger and hate, regardless of its justification, and turns to love, is a forgiving heart. A forgiving heart is one that is receptive to and welcomes the Creator's love - the only and true Source of love. It is a heart through which love can flow between and among us – as intended. Love flowing is a manifestation of Spirit, and serves to awaken the spirit of and within each and all. Trespasses are not acts of the Spirit – thus with Spirit present and active, love continues to enter, continues to flow.

When love is present in the process,
so too is our Creator present...
the Creator whose very essence is love,
and who is the Source,
the Ultimate Source of love...

It is through love being present in the
process that it becomes possible for
"Thy Will" to be done – on this earth,
at this time... this time of potential.

Christ's Two Principles

The first sin, the first act of disobedience, was interfering with the Creator's intended working of life in the world... and the first temptation was the eating of the apple.

In the beginning we did not honor the Creator's intention, and through succumbing to temptation, we entered a path of "my will," not "Thy Will."

Christ left us two principles, *"Love thy Father"* (Cf. Mt 22:37; 6:9), and *"Love one another as Christ loved us"* (Cf. Jn 13:34). Loving thy Father certainly would involve the honoring of the Creator's intention, and the intended working of life in the world. This in a sense would be a perfect reflection of the Creator's love. Loving each other involves seeing and relating to the essence - the pattern of intention - of each other.

Christ, who came to reopen the way, the return to honoring intention and "Thy Will," experienced without faltering, the temptations present while serving "Thy Will", not "my will." In one way, it seems that Christ had to "walk the path" of perfection – experiencing, encountering and surmounting temptation, and choosing "Thy Will" over "my will," so that the path of intention - the path of our potential - could be reopened, made visible and accessible.

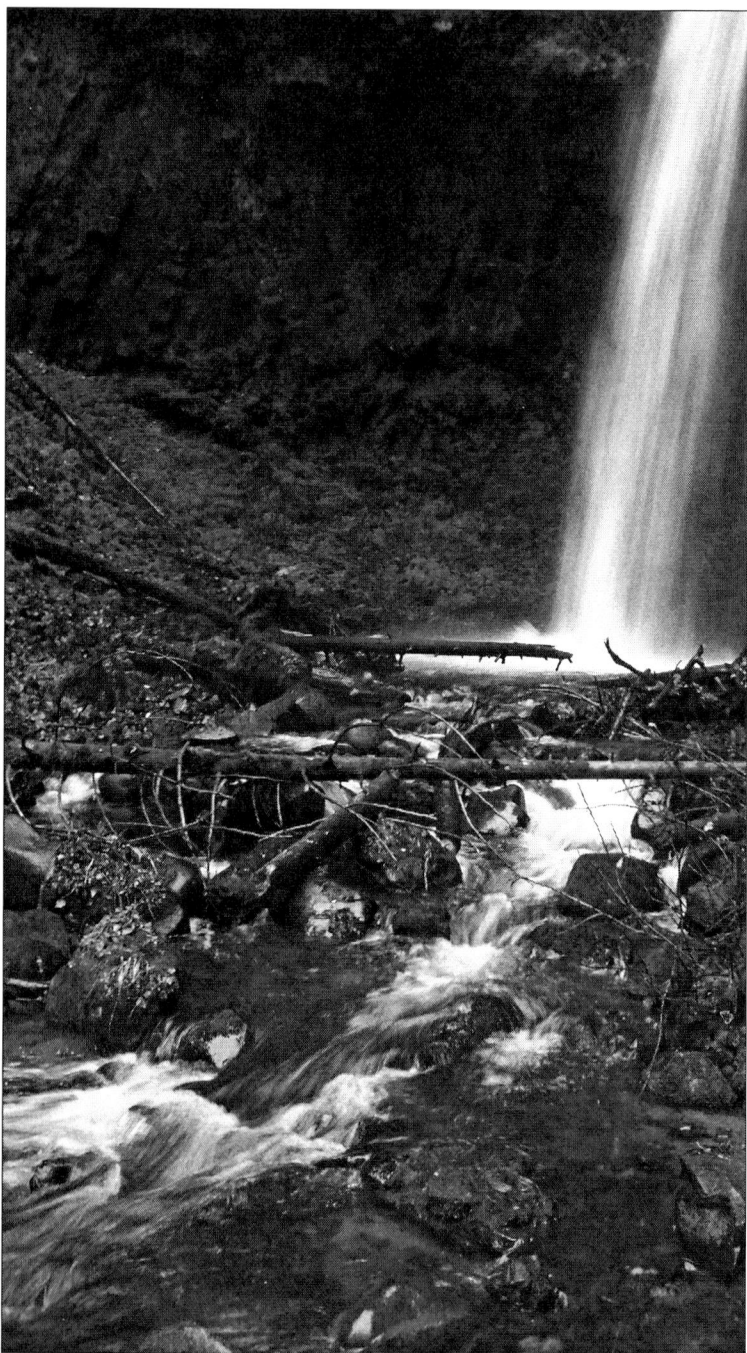

Faith

Oh Great Spirit... Source of creation... Keeper of the mysterious, but knowable intent...

As we work to sustain and nourish our life – the life of our human family – let our actions be guided, not by our likes or our perceived needs and rights, but rather by your intention...

And, as we turn towards your intention... shower us with faith – faith as unceasing as the warmth and love of the sun, giver of life...

> Faith, that if we open our hearts and awaken our conscience, the wisdom present during creation will be revealed...
>
> A faith – that through wisdom revealed – will enable us to join in your intent... in your creation... to fill our roles to do the work you expect...

And help us to willfully and joyfully embrace the truth that hope – ultimate hope for humankind, for human life – lies in right and good works for the whole – the whole of life, for life itself...

Lastly, since it is our common experience to doubt, to question and to favor reason over wisdom... help us see and taste the realness of the revelations and manifestations that emerge from faith in your intent and intended ways of working.

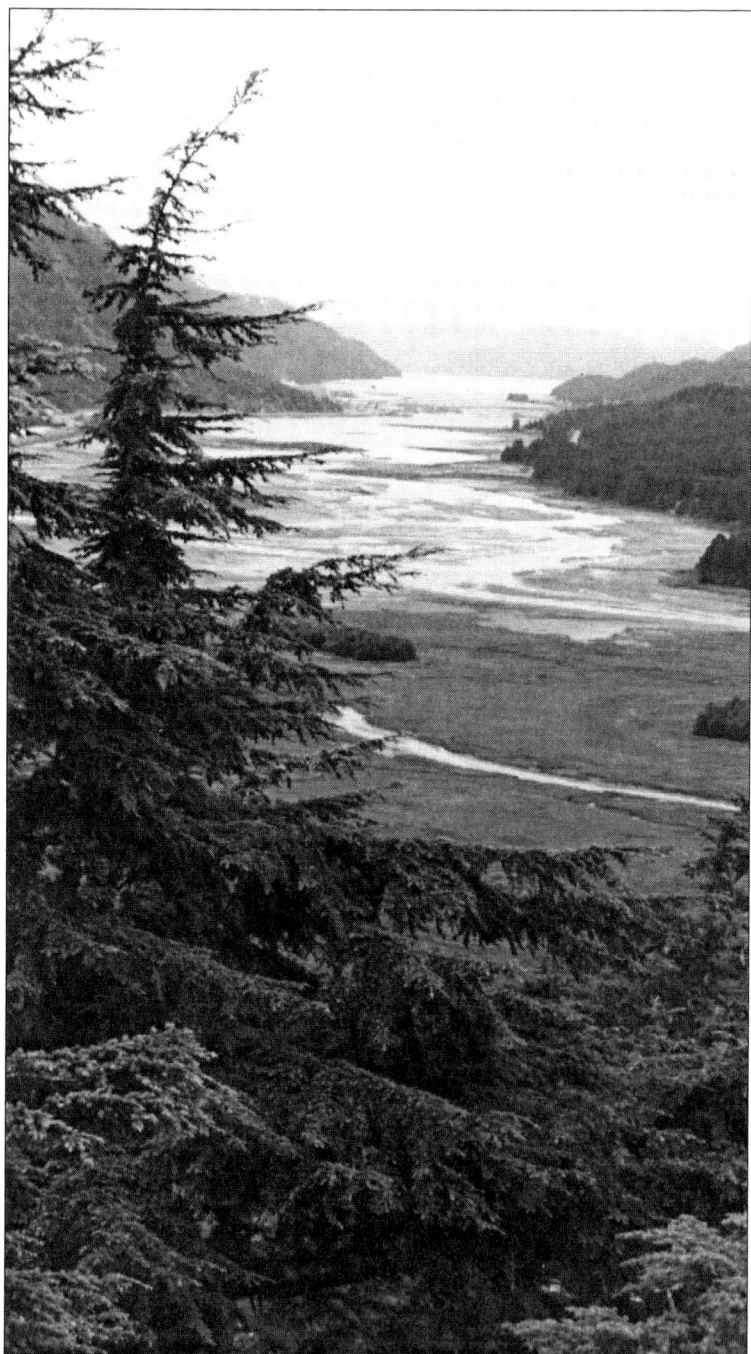

Part 2

Becoming Instruments
for Love Entering

We have faith in the intent and the intended ways of working of the Creator.

We have hope and are hopeful because there lies within us the potential to become fully and truly human.

And beyond that, our spirit is lifted through the understanding that by surrendering ourselves to our instrumentality, love enters the process…

And *with love, all things are possible* (Cf. Mt 19:26; 1Jn 4:8).

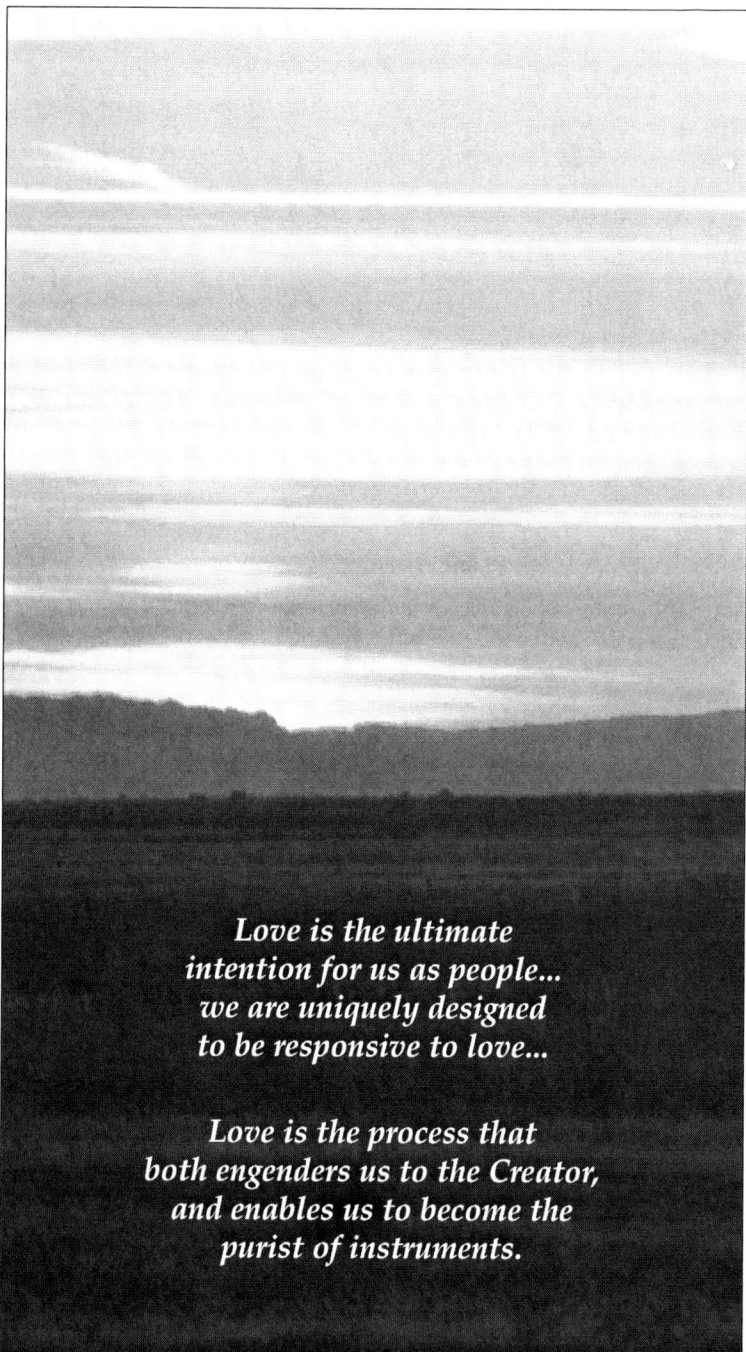

*Love is the ultimate
intention for us as people...
we are uniquely designed
to be responsive to love...*

*Love is the process that
both engenders us to the Creator,
and enables us to become the
purist of instruments.*

Reflecting on the Philosophical Teachings Embedded in the Temptations of Christ

The devil seemingly knew that if Jesus said "Yes" to his instrumentality, love would enter into the creation, making it possible for the full power of the Creator to become present and manifest in the working of the life processes of earth... making possible a transition from a required obedience to commands, to willful surrendering to one's instrumentality: Embrace the love of the Creator rather than act merely in accord with the fear of God. The trick the devil tried on Jesus was to convince him that power is what man is created to pursue such that he could impose on life his wishes, under the illusionary sense of that being the wish of the Creator. The three temptations of Jesus (Ref. Lk 4:1-13) were seductive invitations for Jesus to retreat from the pattern of intent – the intention of the Source.

• *Turn stone into bread to feed yourself* (Cf. Lk 4:3). It is not right to violate the essence pattern of any of life's elements – living or non-living – for personal gain or self-satisfaction.

• *You say you are the Son of God and you have legions of angels behind you - prove there is a God and prove who you are by throwing yourself down from the tower and they will save you* (Cf. Lk 4:9-11). Truth is above proof. Truth is only real when it is present in the heart, and it is through and from the heart that we realize the value of truth. To seek to prove and justify a truth is not the right use of the mind. The mind's work is to act from and be guided by truth as it works to manifest essential structures… structures that come from essence and support essential processes for manifesting spirit. It is wrong to destroy creation to prove there is a Creator. Truth has no meaning unless embraced by the heart; seeking proof only diminishes the realness and meaning of truth.

> • *The devil would give to Christ power over all of creation* (Cf. Lk 4:5-7). Earth belongs to the Creator... it is neither the devil's to give, nor man's to lord over. Pursuing power is the most effective deterrent of love. Pursing power over love begets fear... and the illusion that some are greater than others. In reality, there is the Creator and, except for the Creator, all are equal.

Turning now to the words of Jesus in regards to our temptations...

"Lead us not into temptation" (Cf. Mt 6:13). Lead implies that we are entering into and embracing life... and as we are led into life, we are given the potential of becoming instruments of the Creator. True temptations are those that would keep us from accepting our own instrumentality... and having accepted our instrumentality, being tricked along the path into believing we are the source. The ultimate temptation is the temptation of taking ourselves as the source, for example source of power, source of wisdom, source of love, source of good.

"Forgive us our trespasses" (Cf. Mt 6:12). Pursuit of our instrumentality is a clumsy process which brings with it both unintended and intentional trespasses which tend to be experienced as disturbances by those who are trespassed upon... disturbances that can give rise to reactivity and negativity without necessarily evoking useful reflection... thus the hazard that the tres-

passed may become less receptive, less open, to the intentions of the Creator. Forgive us those trespasses where we are trying to do your work and we evoke negativity – when the mind works to enable us to gain advantage over or position over another.

Be not the source of negative energy; the greatest burden for the whole is the requirement to refine – to remove – the impurities of negative energies, such as anger, jealousy, self-righteousness, divisiveness, etc. Coarse energies clog the arteries - the life-enriching pathways - of the body of life thus making it harder for all the living systems that make up the body. Negative energies, once in our bodies, must be purified out for our being instruments of the ongoing flow of love of the Creator.

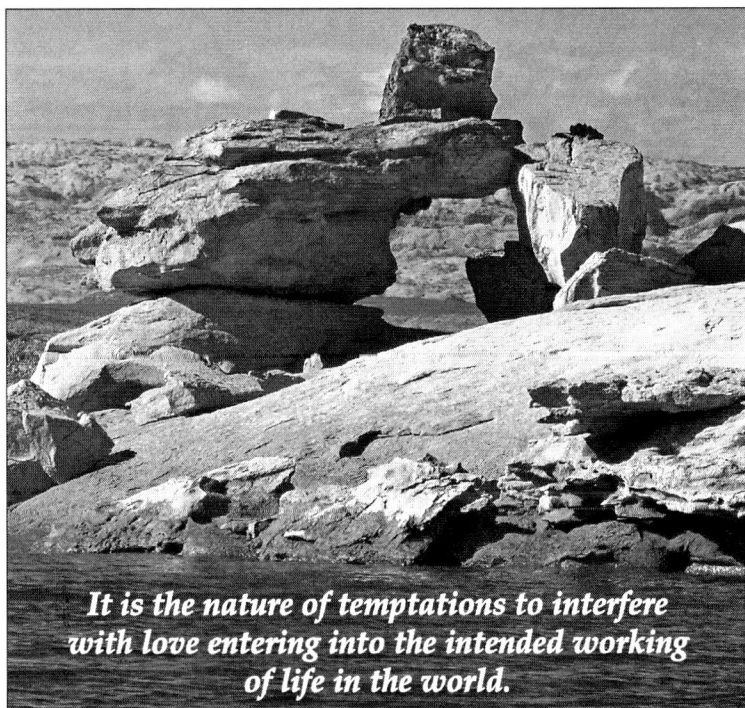

It is the nature of temptations to interfere with love entering into the intended working of life in the world.

Reflecting on the Working of Love

Love... continuously emanates from the Essence of creation, its true and only Source. With unfailing alertness and infinite patience, love seeks an opening through which it can flow... the means by which it can enter into the working of life in the world. In the absence of an open vessel, a receptive heart, love cannot enter the world... and a loveless world ceases to work, ceases to be, and brings unimaginable suffering to its Creator.

Upon entry, love works not to gain power... nor does it pursue power and authority over others; it seeks not to dominate, nor to be understood. Love seeks to illuminate and gain understanding of.

Love casts not shadows... it is pure light... a light that freely enters a receptive heart - a beckoning instrument. Love, once welcomed, goes about its work of reflecting from and among one another... a reflecting that awakens faith, breathes life into hope, and strengthens spirit. Love illuminates ultimate truths... the truth of our instrumentality... the illusion of our being a source... the truth of our oneness and equality... the reality that but for our Creator, no one is superior. Love celebrates our uniqueness as it works to unfold and manifest our essence.

While love holds returning to the Source as its purpose... love has as its ultimate aim lighting the path of evolution of our being... the path by which we ultimately become that which was and is intended: a perfect reflection of the image from and through which we were created. Love enters and lights our path in ways that sustain our longing to return, and our ever-strengthening yearning to become. Always beckoning and occasionally admonishing us along our intended path of progression, love lightens the burden of our soul... yet calls attention to and provides focus to the work before us.

Love lights the way… and leads us to advance our humanness beyond love based on or restricted to common or shared blood… to embrace one another, each and all members of the human family, as brothers and sisters – neighbors, one and all.

As we, humankind, progress along our path, and our capacity for embracing the working of love deepens, our work becomes increasingly intrinsic… requiring more inner acceptance and a freer and more conscious choice not realizable through external forces (for example, authority or persuasion, reason and logical argument, commands, threats, fear or guilt), but more and more through the work of our heart and the working of our conscience. Each new progression does not diminish the significance of the previous, nor lessen it being required… rather, that which comes before becomes enfolded into the new… with deeper and truer meaning, and a greater possibility of being truly lived out. Thus the new progression - to embrace the whole of life, to understand and honor its working, and to nourish and bring forth life's potential and its processes - does not diminish the love required and intended between and among our brothers and sisters… nor does it lessen, but rather makes more real, the truth of our dignity and equality. And, as we continue our progression along our path, love's working calls upon and requires many more, not fewer, receptive hearts and willful instruments… especially now, with oneness and wholeness being brought to the fore. These receptive hearts become the focal points of the light, of that which is to be understood and served… the aim of our work.

Surrendering to Instrumentality

Christ, rather than just reconnecting or regenerating the pathway to love as it was previously manifested, brought to us a resurrecting evolutionary step in the experience of love on earth. He made known that we – each and all – are brothers and sisters, sons and daughters of a Common Father (Ref. Mt 6:9; 12:50)… and that love is to flow within, through, between and among all. Love is to flow freely through receptive and open hearts, unrestrained and unrestricted by blood relationships, the chosen and un-chosen. This is to be an all-inclusive process, open to all who would willfully open their hearts to the Creator… love equally present and available to all – restrained and restricted only by the receptivity of the heart.

This evolution in love makes possible our living and working in the higher ways brought to humankind through Christ. This evolution is not so much physical, material, or functional in nature, but rather one of being. Being evolutions require inner processing… processes that include and involve reflection, conscience, receptivity to wisdom, and, most particularly, openness of and to the heart… and at this time, the surrendering to one's instrumentality and the answering of the call… a process exemplified by Mary, the mother of Jesus (Ref. Lk 1:38).

And, as is true of evolutionary processes, the previously revealed truths of the time of law and obedience are not discarded, but rather enfolded into the new way… enfolded in a way that deepens the meaning of that which was, and spiritually enriches that which is to be and become.

And so, through reflecting on the multifold working of Christ, we can begin to see more clearly the reopening of the pathway to the Father, the reconnecting of the Father's people to the Father, his teachings developing an understanding of a way of life, a way of of manifesting spirit... and by the way of his life and work, revealing to us the truth of our instrumentality... the truth that the Father, our Common Father, is the Source of all good (Cf. Lk 18:19). And at this time, obedience welcomes the truth of our willful surrendering to our instrumentality and the answering of the call. In this way, we, in a manner similar to that of Christ, can make way for the entry and flowing out into the working of the world, the Spirit – such that the intentionality of the Creator can be carried out. Here again we can see the upward shift from being agents of God to becoming instruments... vessels through which the Spirit – the manifesting will of the Creator – can flow. Whereas Mary, by surrendering to her instrumentality (Ref. Lk 1:38), made possible the material realization of Christ, it is through our surrendering that makes possible the spiritual realization of the Christ. And in this way we willfully engage and walk upon the ascending unfolding path of intentionality, the path of our potential.

Being Open to Instrumentality

"Our Father" (Mt 6:9)… We are, each and all, children of one Common Father, our Creator. Our Father is the Source of life, the Creator of life on earth – as well as the universe that contains earth. Our mother, the earth, is the receiver of the Spirit of life continually flowing from our Common Father. Earth is our mother; the Creator is our Father. We – each and all – are brothers and sisters, called by the Father to love each other. By love flowing through us and among us, we become what we were designed and created to become... by love flowing through us, we cooperate with the unfolding of the potential enfolded in the ongoing creation. For love to flow through us, we make a conscious, deliberate and intentional choice to become instruments such that the Creator might do with us as wished... use us as receptive instruments to play our uniquely designed role in the ongoing creation... the aim of which lives with the Father. Making ourselves choiceful receptive instruments, we become able to fulfill our role in the intended and unfolding creation, and by so doing, becoming whole, becoming free, becoming complete. Serving our calling, we experience the freedom and joy, the hope and love that are gifts of the Father. Serving the call, we become fully and truly human... and we manifest spirit, spirit that will be available to all of life on earth forever.

The Prayer to the Father tells us we are not the source, but the instrument. The Source dwells in another world; the will of the Source is done in the kingdom of heaven. Yet it is the intent of the Creator that the will be manifest *"on earth as in heaven"* (Mt 6:10). Earth and life on earth are created to be and become a harmonious living developing whole. We cannot know, for our minds are too small, the aim of this creation called earth. Yet we do know, by the words of Jesus Christ in the teaching prayer to the Father, that we are called to co-operate with the will of the Creator - the will of the Creator for life as a whole on earth – such that earth also becomes a place where the intention of the Creator is made manifest.

There is an intent of creation, a particular yet dramatic way the creation is designed and intended to unfold... and we are, each and all, through the pattern of our essence, designed and intended to fill a role in its unfolding. Yes we have a choice... we can choose to live from the pattern of our essence, opening ourselves to the will and love of the Father, or go another way. Uncertainty, as well, is present to the unfolding of creation itself, an unfolding that at the very least relies in part on our willfulness to be open to our instrumentality. Will we make the choice, not just once but ongoingly, out of love, to do "Thy Will"? Will we drink the cup of our calling with our hearts open to the love of the Creator?

*Transcending the
ego of identity,
we enter into
the early stages
of the path of
intentionality.*

Our Reason for Being

The "ruler" of this world is "my will." When we pursue "my will" we have no freedom; our choice, our soul, is lost, for the "my" of "my will" is the ego, not the essence – not the pattern of intent of our Creator - the essence being the heart of the Father's gift to us as we are given life. Our essence is not loud and clamoring. It waits quietly to speak, to speak of our purpose. For what reason did we come into the world? What is our *"hour"* (Ref. Jn 12:27)? And then, what unfolding, what becoming, is essential to prepare for that hour? We are called to answer "Yes" to that for which we were designed, that for which we were intended, that to which we are called, "Yes" to the essence held in our heart of hearts.

A True Instrument of Co-Creation

Thus it came to be that Mary, through her willful surrendering, prayerful beckoning, pure and receptive heart, made possible the manifestation, the material realization of Jesus... the particular manifestation required for the time. This willful surrendering to one's instrumentality – not "my will" but "Thy Will" (Ref. Lk 1:38) – was the foretelling of a new time: a new way of being and becoming... a new way that would be made visible and practiced through the works and teachings of Jesus the Christ, and through the working of the Spirit after the ascension of Christ into heaven.

Mary became an instrument of co-creation by fulfilling a particular role of willful cooperation with the intended working of the creation. It is through this way of surrendering, being of open heart and cooperating, that we can become co-creators – instruments of co-creation... vessels required for the entry and working of the Spirit in the world - the instrumental means through which the Spirit carries out the unfolding intent of the Creator.

Christ himself became an instrument for the will of the Father (Ref. Mt 26:39), an instrument that not only made salvation – the reuniting of ourselves with our Common Father – possible, but also put in place the process of becoming: the way by which we could become that which – through intentionality – we have the potential to become and be... perfected instruments for the working of the Spirit... living and fulfilling the work of roles of significance.

Open Our Hearts

Oh good and gentle Father,
Creator of life and work,
Look down with mercy upon your children.
Let your love overflow in the river of human dignity.
Open our hearts to the hearts of others.
Open our hearts to the created essence…
> Of all children, all families, all neighbors, all
> communities.
> Of all lands, all countries, all peoples, and of
> earth itself.

Open our hearts to the oneness of humanity, and the
wholeness of life on earth.
> Help us, Oh Lord, to be able to see the essential
> beauty of every facet of your unfolding
> creation.

Make us instruments in the work of your ongoing
creation.

Part 3

Accessing
Going Forward Wisdom

At the beginning of the beginning, or perhaps even before,

There was intent...

An intent out from which flows the knowable, intentional word,

And the seeable unfolding creation...

Wisdom, accessible wisdom, was present to intent...

And accessible wisdom is ongoingly present to the unfolding,

The unfolding of the word and of the creation.

Going Forward Wisdom

The path of salvation, the way of salvation, has been open to us – each and all – since the time of Christ. At the time of Christ, the search for a path to salvation came to a close – a definitive close. The closing of the search - it no longer being necessary - and the establishment, the permanent presence, of the path of salvation were the good news, the truly good news... good news made possible by Christ saying "Yes," by his death, resurrection and returning to the Father... and by completing the cycle of work, the work required to return us to the path of our potential, the potential we were endowed with, intentionally endowed with at the time of our creation... the potential to become fully and truly human... a potential made real and seemingly realized by him through his process, his life on earth.

Christ, no doubt intentionally, in addition to his teachings in regard to the path of salvation, gave us some going forward wisdom, some intentional commands and processes, all of which in one way or another have yet to be fully embraced and lived out. This going forward wisdom and these commands were – by his words (Ref. Mt 5:17-18) - in no way intended to diminish the law expressed before his coming. Thus the continued relevance of obedience, and the knowing of what is meant by the word – the word of God - and the realness and necessity of the experience of being sorrowful, of asking for forgiveness for infractions, acts of disobedience, etc., all of which may cause us to "fall out of grace" - the good grace of God, the redeeming grace made possible and forever present by the salvation work of Christ.

This path of salvation, an inclusive path, a path clearly open to each and all who would choose it, is an accomplished reality... a reality that makes possible the embracing and walking along the path of potential... a path that acknowledges the truth that if love is not present in the process, love will not be present in the outcome... a path illuminated by, and pointed to by the going forward wisdom and intentional commands of Christ... a wisdom and intention given to all who would choose this path, not just those present at the time it was given. Some of the essential going forward expressions being:

• *"Love God,"* and *"Love one another as I have loved you"* (Cf. Mt 22:37; Jn 13:34), greatly enhanced by a practice-able philosophy

• His prayer to the Father (Ref. Mt 6:9-15) – the prayer Jesus gave us, a way for us to pray after his return to the Father... a prayer in which each and all of us are recognized as sharing a Common Father – a Common Source.

• The wisdom that *"Whose sins you forgive are forgiven them, and whose sins you retain are retained"* (Jn 20:23)... the wisdom that our retaining of sins - our not forgiving trespasses - interferes with, at times blocks, love entering into the process – into the working of the world... as intended, as necessary for the intended unfolding.

• The Beatitudes (Ref. Mt 5:3-12) – a way of inner processing not commonly understood, or seemingly actively present.

As we begin to see the complementary nature of the path of salvation and the going forward path of potential – the path of intention -, we bring to mind an observation expressed in a variety of ways by a number of people through time – that faith without philosophy risks becoming a myth[10]... a working truth that becomes more understandable as we see that faith, with its emphasis on the word, commonly has the character of meaning and obedience – seeking meaning, striving to obey. Philosophy, in particular the living philosophy of potential, has the character of understanding and discipline – understanding the essential working of something, and developing a discipline, being disciplined – disciples - in that regard.

In addition, the salvation side leans toward the hereafter, whereas the living philosophy of potential leans toward the here and now – unique, but complementary perspectives, both of which emanate from the innermost urges of our design: our longing to return to the Source, and our yearning to become – to become fully and truly human, to fulfill our potential, becoming instruments of love fully participating in the intended unfolding. It is this yearning to become that is now active at this time of potential – this time of going forward, of moving towards wholeness… a time made visible and enabled by the living philosophy of potential… a philosophy that begins with the truth that if love is not present in the process, love will not be present in the outcome… a philosophy necessary for taking up and carrying out the work of re-connecting to, of taking direction from, intent – the intended way of working –, the intent that preceded, came before the word and the works… a philosophy that requires a life of the whole perspective, a perspective that acknowledges our living nature, a perspective necessary for our moving towards wholeness, for our living in harmony with life's processes, a perspective essential to developing the ethics and ethicality required to advance our humanness, and to transcend the seemingly impossible barriers and deep divisiveness present before us today.

"Our Father" at this Time of Potential

"Our Father" (Mt 6:9) recognizes we – each and all – have a Common Father. We are not merely a collection of individuals; we are intended to be one working whole, with each having a part to fill. We are all brothers and sisters. And we are not the source… there is one Source: our Common Father.

"In heaven" (Mt 6:9) makes real the all in all of intentionality. Heaven – intentionality – was before the word – the revealed word - and before the works – the unfolding creation. *"Our Father in heaven"*… our Common Father is the fullness of intentionality.

"Hallowed be Thy name" (Mt 6:9). Name is being sanctified… the name of God the Father… the name, "I AM." The Father is all being… the Father is love. Can we be surprised, therefore, that Jesus, who gave us this prayer, also gave us a new Commandment, a Commandment essential to the end of the age, that being *"Love one another even as I love you"* (Jn 13:34)? This Commandment tells us the way in which we are hallowing the name of the Father, hallowing the essence of the Father… which is love.

"Thy kingdom come… on earth as in heaven" (Mt 6:10). Here we petition the Father – our Common Father – for his kingdom of heaven to manifest on earth. We call, we pray, for his full intentionality – for the fulfillment of his intended unfolding of the enfolded creation. Our wish is to live on earth in the full process of the unfolding intentionality of our Common Father. This would be peace among people; this would be harmony with the life processes of earth; this would be *"Thy kingdom… on earth as in heaven."*

"Thy will be done on earth as in heaven" (Mt 6:10). We pray to our Father with no doubt that his will is done in heaven… and knowing full well, because we

know to some degree our own hearts and minds, and the hearts and minds of others, that the will of the Father is scantily being done on earth. And so we call the Father to give us the grace to answer "Yes" to his call… to take our part in his unfolding intent on this earth. We pray he will guide and help us become instruments of love, the instruments essential to heaven on earth… the instrumentality essential to our shifting from being "only human" to becoming fully and truly human… the instrumentality – the giving up "my will" to "Thy Will" - essential to becoming fully and truly human, thus taking up our role in forming the soul of humanity.

"*Give us this day our daily bread*" (Mt 6:11). Jesus said, "*My food is to do the will of the one who sent me*" (Jn 4:34). If we have quieted ourselves to hear our call, to hear "Thy Will"… the call to be sent – sent to fill our role in the intended unfolding -, and answer "Yes" to our calling, then we need, each day, food. And what is this food? Our Father gives us, through the Spirit, guidance we need to harmonize with and fill our role in his unfolding creation of life on earth… and when we fulfill his will, when we "see" and follow the path he gives, then we are fed. Our food is the doing of the work of "Thy Will."

The second part of the prayer to the Father guides our work, guiding us and protecting us as we take up our particular work and role in unfolding the potential enfolded before the beginning – unfolding the potentiality of the intent of our Common Father. The first part asks for a "seeing" of and faith in intentionality - the enfolded potential - knowing that as we take our part in its unfolding, we will receive our daily bread: "*My food is to do the will of the one who sent me*" (Jn 4:34).

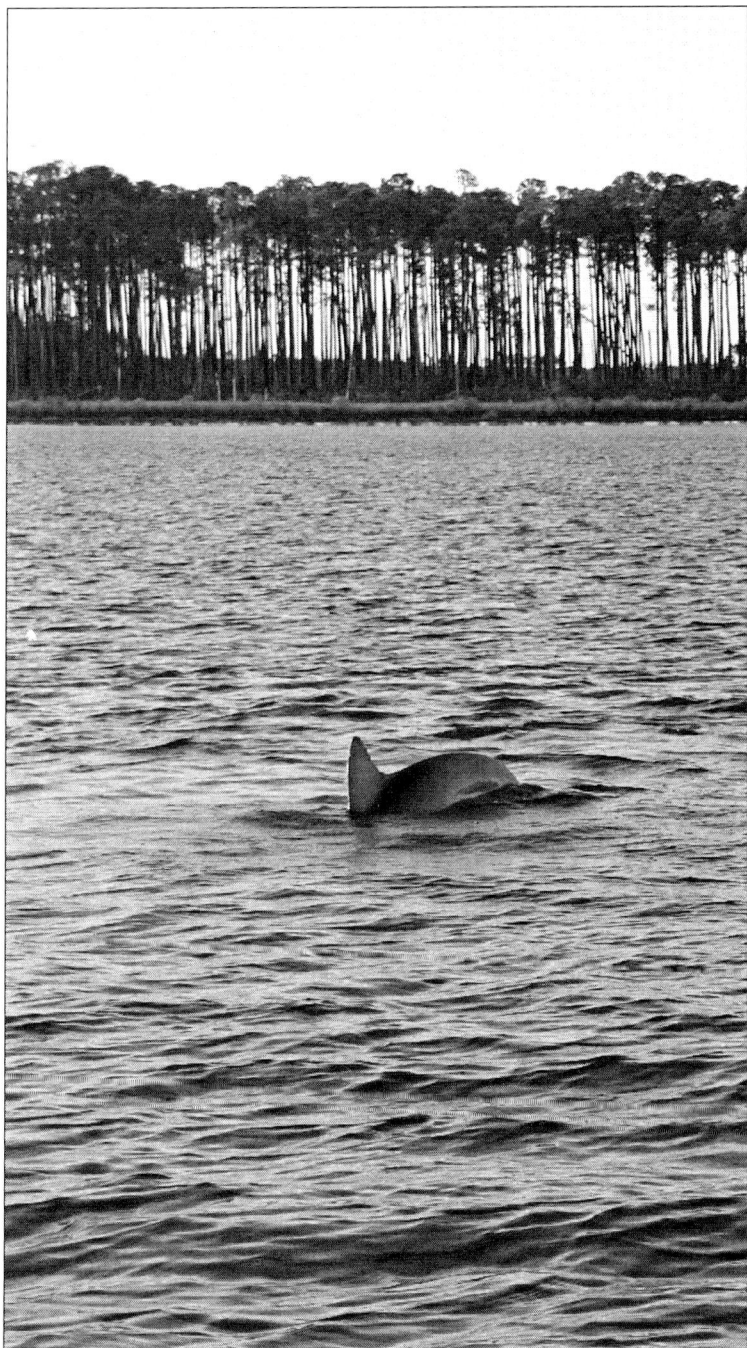

Our acting from
and through
intended instrumentality is
a manifestation of
"Thy Will"
being done on this earth...
at this time.

Through the Narrow Gate

Mary's surrender (Ref. Lk 1:38) was an act of pure faith - faith that transcended the fear of consequences - and was unreluctantly open to what she could not see. She surrendered to an opening, without seeing what was to be unfolded for herself or her son. Jesus (Ref. Mt 26:38-46), on the other hand, seemed to clearly know to what he was saying "Yes"; he understood the cup of which he was to drink, the cup of "Thy Will," not "my will."

Christ was truly the first to go through the narrow gate and complete the journey... the journey to pure essence - the process of manifesting Spirit, the Spirit essential to intended unfolding - the journey to the realization of potential, the fulfilling of intent and intended ways of working. He finished the race along the path that is now open to the many – all who willfully choose... a path to community, the true soul of humanity, the whole necessary for human spirit - the essence of humanity - to be manifested, such that our (humankind's) work and role in the intended unfolding can be carried out... and as always, a time of great hazard.

"I am the way, and the truth and the life" (Jn 14:6). The Beatitudes (Ref. Mt 5:3-12) are the way – the inner map - to the narrow gate... the entrance to the path, the path made clear by Christ; the experience of the path being "lifted up" by the latter Beatitudes... the particular journey not yet seeable – thus (like Mary) a true act of faith – faith that transcends the fear of the knowable consequences, and faith that willfully surrenders to a yet unseen path... a path not of our making, but a path we are called to follow.

The Way of Love and Peace

To begin, *"Seeing the crowds, he went up the mountain"* (Mt 5:1)… up the mountain to a higher level than the world of material.. up the mountain to access the world of Spirit… up the mountain where wisdom enters.

"His disciples came near to him" (Mt 5:1)… those whose wish it was to work, to work from the world of Spirit, to access the Spirit and to manifest spirit in the world.

"He began to teach them" (Mt 5:2)… there is a teaching… a disciplined process, an intentional process… showing a way of innerly organizing ourselves… revealing the inner work to be done such that we are able to fulfill the call to manifest spirit in community by taking on the work of intentional purpose – purpose that reflects our part in the unfolding intentionality.

"Blessed are the poor in spirit, because of them is the kingdom of heaven" (Mt 5:3).

Being poor in spirit, we accept there is only one Source… the Creator. Being poor in spirit, we let go of seeing self as the source… and turn our hearts to the one true Ultimate Source. Being poor in spirit, we are given access to faith… faith in intentionality and the rightness and goodness of the intended unfolding.

"Blessed are they who are mourning, for they shall be comforted" (Mt 5:4).

Letting go of self as source - self as having spiritual possessions - we mourn our loss, yet mourning our loss, we enter a reflective state, one in which we begin to see the Creator's love... we begin to see intentionality... the unfolding creation intended... a "seeing" that gives us hope. We mourn the loss of our self-made goals, visions and plans, our cultural "shoulds" and "oughts," and our imagined control – all those things of existence, of "my will," to which we are attached and with which we identify - and are comforted by the truth of and confidence in the unfolding intent and intended ways of working of creation... the truth of the ever-flowing love of the Creator accessible by receptive hearts, hearts yearning to become instruments.

"Blessed are the meek, because they shall inherit the earth" (Mt 5:5).

The condition of and for inheriting the earth – responsibility for the earth – is meekness, gentleness. Meek is the shift to not "my will," but "Thy Will." Meekness, gentleness is the quality of interaction with the life processes of earth expected of those who have inherited it, who will inherit it. For through meekness, we become able to harmonize with the ongoing intended and unfolding creation of life on earth, more able to advance our humanness, to fulfill our role in and through life, the life of all, the whole of life.

"Blessed are those who are hungering and thirsting after righteousness, because they shall be satisfied" (Mt 5:6).

With this hunger and thirst, we enter into a transforming fire, for this is a hunger and thirst that can be quenched, can be filled, only by fulfilling the Creator's intentionality. We hunger and thirst for fulfilling the Creator's intent. The first three Beatitudes (our striving for letting go of self as source and embracing the Creator as the one and only Source; our seeing there are intended ways of working in the ongoing unfolding creation; our shifting to and seeing the strength in the meekness of not "my will," but "Thy Will") are all working at preparing our hearts to experience an insatiable hunger and thirst for an ongoing unfolding intentional role and purpose in the unfolding creation... a hunger and thirst for seeing and embracing the role and work, the intended purpose towards which we are drawn, drawn by and through our unique essence – the pattern of intention.

"Blessed are the merciful, because they shall receive mercy" (Mt 5:7).

Reflecting innerly in regards to our efforts relative to this path, this way of love and peace, we notice at times we are hesitating, wandering, going astray, and at times we are embracing, truly working, etc. We also notice that as we begin to see, to gain a glimmer of the intent and intended ways of working of the unfolding creation, of the unfolding life of the whole, we are often tempted to judging - judging of others... and of ourselves as well. With judging comes much hazard – judging can effectively interfere with love entering and flowing through. We cannot know the inner struggle of another, the undeclared purposes they hold, the inner nature of their effort... we can, through our experience, understand the depth of striving required of this path, the necessity of community – particularly at this time of potential – for our progressing as a person, as a people… thus the turning towards mercy, accessing and living from mercy. Jesus was merciful to those who were not his disciples; Jesus was merciful to all – a process of continuous flowing of love, of caring about. Being merciful, being present to mercy, is an essential characteristic of entering – and re-entering – this path, the way of love and peace. It is through mercy, and being merciful that we recognize and honor the truth of our equality – of our being, at essence, equal – equally endowed with intentionality, commonly called to instrumentality… truths that themselves become the forming core for community – a community embracing a further truth that if love is not present in the process, love will not be present in the outcome.

"Blessed are the pure in heart, because they shall see God" (Mt 5:8).

Our hearts, when striving to experience and be present to the hearts of others, a striving made possible by our detaching from "my will," begin to develop a seeing – eyes of the heart – that recognize and embrace the presence of God in others. More and more we become able to see the potential enfolded within the unique essence of each and of all… an essence yearning to be manifested as a working living part – an essential role, an enabling spirit – in the intended unfolding life of the whole.

"Blessed are the peacemakers, because they shall be called children of God" (Mt 5:9)

Embracing our instrumentality - surrendering to our instrumentality - love enters the process... we are becoming instruments of love. When we fully embrace our instrumentality and take up our role in the community, the community is becoming an instrument of love. Love enters the process... the unfolding of intentionality is becoming real... the community is fulfilling its intended role in the flow of love into, through and out from the earth... the community is becoming a maker of peace, a peace that can be further unfolded and manifested throughout the world.

Thus peace, the companion and partner to love, joins in the process of returning love to the Father Creator... and they – the followers of the way of love and peace - are becoming and being called children of God, known by their way of living and working.

"Blessed are they being persecuted because of righteousness, for of them is the kingdom of heaven" (Mt 5:10).

The kingdom of heaven is coming into being through working for the sake of fulfilling "Thy Will," fulfilling the intentionality of the Creator. Being persecuted by the world is a common experience of those taking up this work. The "my will" inner and outer world hates the doing of "Thy Will"... and works to sever, through worldly consequences, the intentionality. Through the earlier Beatitude of righteousness, images emerged that bring to life the intentional and that aspect of intentionality that we are particularly drawn to. This work of the heart enables us to enter community and live and work in ways more harmonious with intent. Intentionality on our part is not necessarily warmly and joyously received by the established patterns and norms of current existing culture and current ways of doing things. This harmoniousness with intent is inherent within – essential to – the kingdom of heaven coming to earth. Living and working from the intentionality to which we are drawn, we begin to experience the kingdom of heaven on earth.

"Blessed are you when they shall reproach you, and persecute you, and shall say every evil word against you, lying, on account of me. Rejoice and be very glad, for the reward of you shall be great in heaven; for they thus persecuted the prophets before you" (Mt 5:11-12).

It should not be surprising, as we strive to do "Thy Will," that is, ensure that love is in the process, that the "my will" world reacts negatively to our efforts. Rather, we can rejoice and be glad knowing we are on path as long as we maintain our authenticity in regards to love in the process… for with love in the process, through community, we can experience a deepening oneness with the Source and with each other as one people of earth, and an increased ableness for moving towards wholeness, away from that which divides… we can experience the oneness and wholeness - the intended unfolding at this time of potential.

Judging and Pride

Reflecting on the Beatitudes (Ref. Mt 5:3-12) while holding an orientation towards process, we experience a way - an ongoingness - along the path of our instrumentality… and the seeing of how necessary are gifts – gifts of grace, gifts of mercy – to our sustaining and progressing along this path, a path we must willfully walk, but one which in truth, without gifts, is beyond our capacity, but not beyond what is intended.

…The gift of our being absolved of judging, of being free from any duty to stand in judgment of others… a gift without confusion, given the clarity of the instruction - truly a command - *"to not judge, lest we be judged"* (Mt 7:1). Being absolved of judging is truly a gift in that we see the hazard, the real risk to ourselves and to the integrity of the process itself: the risk of pride entering… a pride which emanates from self love, a self love that leads to the imagining that we are the source of good – of our own "goodness" or the good that we may be associated with or present to… a pride that quickly shields us from the Source - the one, the only, the true Source of love, of good and of truth… a pride that blinds us to the truth that each and all are called along this path, that in truth we cannot know the inner struggles and process of another; and that judging, as we have been instructed, is joyfully unnecessary – outside of our domain – needing no effort or attention on our part.

As this reflection begins to diminish, to come to a close, the notion of humility emerges… the notion of authentic, necessary, and most useful, humility… a true reflection of truth and reality… an enabling stance towards the truth – the truth of our not being the source, not being the source of love, goodness, or truth itself… rather the truth of our intended instrumentality... of the intention for our becoming an instrument for love, truth, and good to enter into the working of the world – as intended, as required for the intended unfolding.

Forming the Soul of Humanity

The manifested will of the Creator is actively and busily at work...

tirelessly and unceasingly working to advance the work of the unfolding creation.

This work is work we cannot do, but work that cannot be done unless we are...

are what we need to be such that Spirit, and therefore love, can enter into and flow through the life processes of earth...

We are being called not to be in control of nor to have control over, but rather to cooperate with; not so much to lead, but rather to be led – led by the images that enter the heart receptive to wisdom, and guided by the light of our conscience.

This work demands unbending resolve and ever deepening patience on our part, for this work holds as its aim an unfolding with which we are fully able to cooperate.

But also this work is one which we, as of yet, lack the capacity to fully envision, to see the whole, and the processes therein...

This is work not of the one, but of the many.

Hope is active and entering all those with receptive hearts – hearts that long to become instruments, hearts that are striving to be free of the illusion of being the source.

As hope enters and establishes its flowing through presence, images and envisionments born of love become visible and accessible – images that make possible the seeing of our role, our path, and the clarifying of our work... work that is both a manifestation of essence, and the hopeful intent of our Creator...

While the whole of that which is to be brought about is not yet visible to us, what is being illuminated is the process of forming the soul of humanity.

This is the work that is required for humankind – the human race – to become fully and truly human, and thereby capable of fulfilling its intended role in the working of the world.

This soul forming work – this effort to prepare us for our intended role – calls upon the uniqueness of each and all, and requires the working and manifesting of spirit through our essence.

This is the means; this is the process; this is the work before us...

Let us pray that we will not be tempted by illusions of "being the source," of being "in charge of," nor by the pursuit of "control over."

May our faith in the intent and intended ways of working of the Creator ever strengthen and grow imperturbably within us.

May we have the strength of resolve that becomes possible only through the desire to carry out "Thy Will."

May the Spirit and love of the Creator find ever increasing numbers of receptive hearts to enter and to flow through...

such that the love required for manifesting the intentional unfolding is truly present.

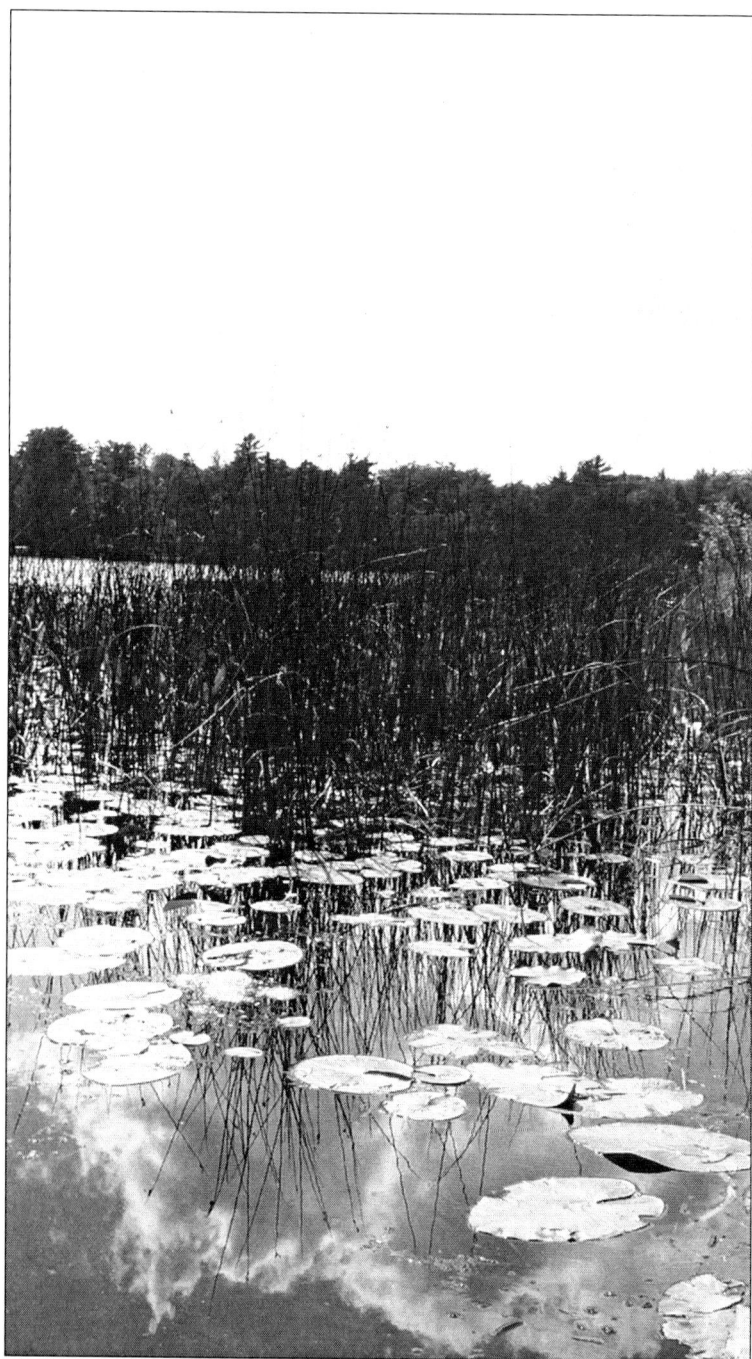

Part 4

America's "YES"

At this time of potential, we the people need to come together...

>   in ways that move us towards wholeness
>   and away from that which divides...
>   in ways that work for all children...
>   all children on earth.

And we need to intentionally work on purpose... on our intentional purpose,
>   our working philosophy, and our ethical
>   principles...

It is time to go forward, to reflectively go forward in ways that advance our humanness...
>   advancing to become a true human community,
>   a living whole...
>   an intentionally working community, working
>   at enriching life...
>   the life of the whole, and the whole of life on
>   this earth.

Life Itself Is...

Life is participatory...

Each and all of its members have a part to play, roles to take up, work to carry out... a gift to bring to the process, a spirit to manifest.

Life is systemic...

Life is therefore purposeful; each and all have purpose, purpose in regards to larger wholes, purposes that lift up the intimate relatedness of one to another... purposes that illuminate intended ways of working, and the truth that "if you touch one, you touch them all"... the truth of community and inseparability.

Life is intentional...

Life emanates from a will force, the Source and force of intention... of intentional ways of being and doing, intent that brings truth, meaning and life to purpose, to purposefulness... a purposefulness that draws Spirit into and through it... through it into the working of the world... as intended.

Life is continuously unfolding...

Life, propelled by the urge of will, works through essence patterns of intent to continuously unfold... an unfolding that is building towards the image, the image held deep within and emerging from the Source... the image of potential, the realization of the intent... the intent that preceded the beginning, the beginning of the word, of the works, the manifestation of the Creator... the beginning of the unfolding... an unfolding that is cyclical, systemic, progressively upward, and spiritual... a manifestation of living through the Spirit, of manifesting spirit... of being forever entwined, present and accessible, in the ongoingness of life itself.

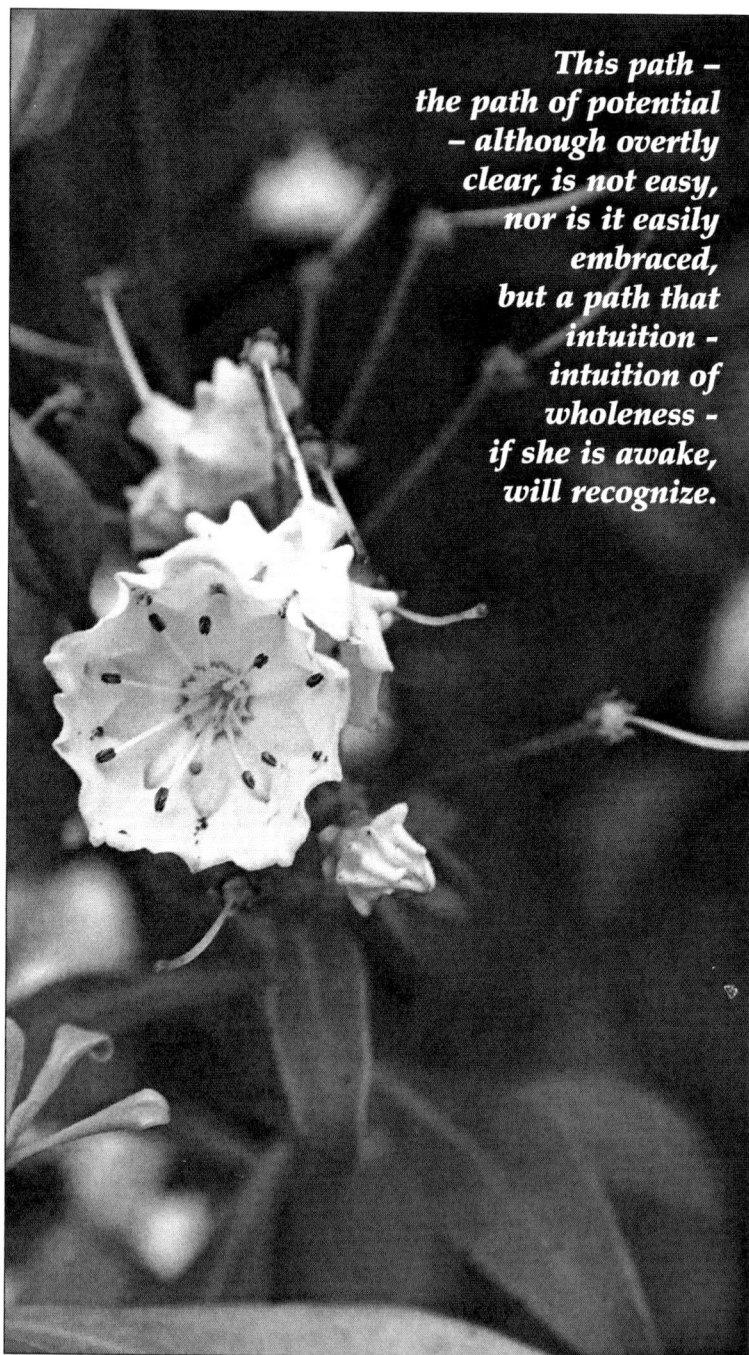

*This path –
the path of potential
– although overtly
clear, is not easy,
nor is it easily
embraced,
but a path that
intuition -
intuition of
wholeness -
if she is awake,
will recognize.*

At This Time... This Time of Potential

Before the beginning there was intention, intention out from which flows the ongoing unfolding of the universe; earth and humankind, the people of earth, were created – came into being – for a purpose.

At this time, this time of great faith, there is a stirring, a genuine calling, for humankind – each and all – to join in the resurrecting of this process of intention – of fulfilling the purpose and role of humankind... purpose that serves the unfolding along the path of our becoming fully and truly human.

At this time, this time of potential, this time of a significant shift – a true step, an authentic leap of faith along our path of becoming fully and truly human - we are being called in a particular way... a way that requires:

- *Wisdom lighting our intended path...* a path of realizing the potential of humankind... a path of fulfilling the intent and intended ways of working of our Creator.

- *Being open to a new perspective...* a life of the whole perspective... a perspective calling upon intuition, the intuition of wholeness... a perspective of seeing, enabling and manifesting essence.

- *Taking on purposes...* purposes that reflect virtue, virtue of the land... purposes that honor and access spirit, spirit of the people... purposes that emerge from the work of the heart, the heart of humanity... intentional purposes.

- *Repotentializing essential processes...* processes of salvation and returning... processes of developing and becoming... essential life processes, and processes of life.

As we strive to take on this repotentializing work, this soul building work of humanity, we will be confronted with the reality that the ultimate unfolding – that which we are being called to join with, to enable – is beyond our grasp. Thus we will experience a demand for trust… trust in the Creator's intent and intended ways of working.

There is, however, that which we can be absolutely certain of: If we reflect on our role, ultimately it is to be an instrument for love to enter into the working of the world… for love is the ultimate expression and manifestation of intention – the original intention… the very essence of the Source.

Thus by being vigilant to ensure that love is present in the process, we can, with conviction and confidence, be assured that love will be present in the outcome – in our purposes and choices along the path of intention… the path of realizing our potential… the path of enabling the intended unfolding.

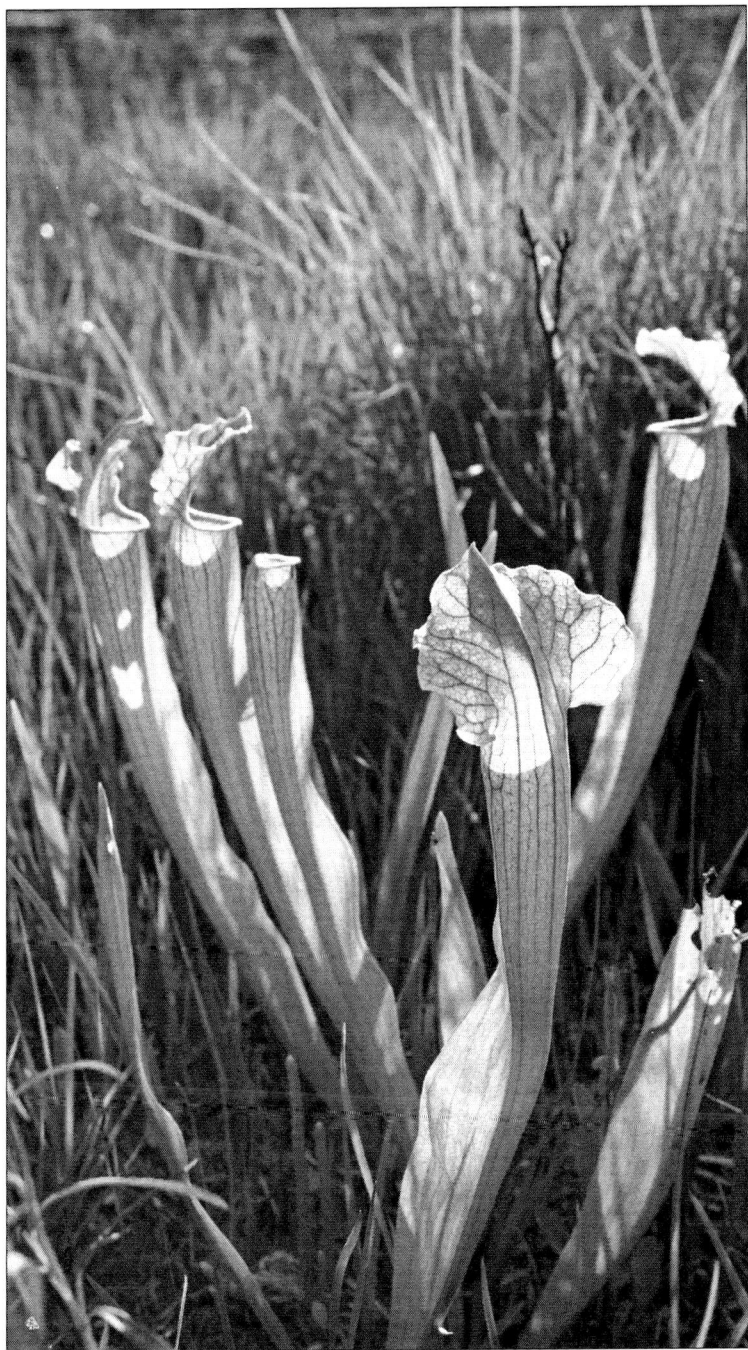

The living philosophy of potential enables the development of the working philosophy for going forward as a people, as a country.

Working Philosophy

Working philosophy is what forms the void – the instrumentality – for love to enter the process. The working philosophy is always about love – compassion. It is where love enters into the process such that Spirit is both being accessed and manifested. We as human beings "quit working" when Spirit drops out... when we operate in un-intended ways. Working philosophy guides the unfolding of – leads to the "seeing" of - intentional purposes. The interesting thing about intentional purposes is that they allow us to enter larger processes - whole systems - through an elemental segment; there is no need to shift the whole (more specifically work on the whole), but rather to focus on entering through a segment. It is somewhat like "the camel getting his nose under the tent" – or perhaps emphasizing "getting healthy" as a response to the issue of health care. Quite a strategy.

This time of potential is a time for shifting – shifting from reactive thinking to reflective thoughtfulness... and through love in the process, shifting our start points from economics, legality and rights to dignity, potential and life of the whole... all of which come together in intentional purposes.

114

Re-Purposing

Ultimately, all purposes are sourced in our Creator's intentionality - the intended ways of our working and living upon this earth. Our work at this time of potential is to generate an understanding and articulation of intentional purposes, intentional purposes being the harmonious integration of the Creator's intent with the intent we hold for systems and processes essential to our well being and continued presence on this earth... and by so doing, we continue our advancement towards becoming more fully and truly human... as intended.

Re-purposing begins with reflective work, reflection and reflective dialogue that have as their aim, the seeing and experiencing of what is actively present when we are truly working – doing the work of our heart... what we commonly think of as our called work. We are drawn to this reflective process as we are experiencing a "coming apart" within ourselves and within our way of working, our way of being... a "coming apart" that is clearly having a de-spiritualizing effect.

Through this reflective work, images come to us, images through which we gain a personal deeper sense of what we are about here, a deeper sense of the virtue within... images which we begin to describe with words... words that express the potential we "see" for re-purposing ourselves and our work... a re-purposing that is possible through the vivification of the essence of our work – our *intentional purpose* - and a *working philosophy* that allows us to both live from and access Spirit. From and through this philosophy and purpose, we begin to unfold our *ethical principles*, principles that enable us to transcend ego – the ego of identity; and ethical principles enable us to stay on course, so to speak, in regards to our purpose... to our being purposeful. We also see within our ethical principles the potential to manage reactivity.

115

This Time of Potential...
A Time of Great Faith

Reflecting on faith, the working of faith...

when faith is actively present in our ways of living and working, we notice...

that as faith becomes increasingly present, fear diminishes...

and as fear increases, faith diminishes...

and further, fear diminished by faith makes possible the entry of love, of love being in the process...

of our ways of living and working being sourced in love...

love bolstered by faith and strengthened by dissipating fear.

This dissipation of fear becomes most real for us as we heartfully and willfully embrace – have faith in, place great faith in – the intent and intended ways of working of our Creator...

faith that we can come together as a people, as a community, and generate disciplined ways of being and behaving...

faith that we can image and create intentional purposes, purposes that reflect our intention and intended ways of working...

and further, faith that we as a community, inspirited

by a new seeing and understanding of the working of discipline and intentionality, can commit to the ethics - the ethical principles - required for this particular effort and work...

a commitment that demands a receptive willfulness of each and all, yet one that can only be lived out through the support and cooperation present within an intentionally working community.

Reflecting on the above, it is quite natural to experience a bit of hesitation, a reluctance, or an inner questioning of the nature a "leap of faith" engenders. Our questioning concerns become transcendable, however, through the confidence and trust that emerge from the embracing of revealed, experienceable, seeable truths...

the truth of our not being the source, but rather we share a Common Source...

the truth of the presence, the manifested presence, of intent – of intentionality, and intended ways of working...

the truth of our being established in good standing with the Source, established such that we can, if we so choose, step out from the shadow - the darkness of fear - and boldly step into the light of love.

The light of love illuminates the truth of the path of intention, the path of our potential to become fully and truly human...

the path of our equality, where each and all are equal in essence...

each having potential, a gift to bring, work to do, roles to take on and live out...

always remembering that if love is not present in the process, love will not be present in the outcome; and remembering as well that as love diminishes, we are ever so cleverly drawn along the way towards darkness - the darkness of fear –, away from the light, and off the path of love...

the path of love being the path along which *through love all things are possible* (Cf. Mt 19:26; 1Jn 4:8)...

a path sustained through faith - true faith – and hope, the genuine hope that intention, harmony with intent, brings to life...

a path and a way of discipline we can approach and pursue without fear...

a path we can walk along and truly *be not afraid* (Cf. Jn 14:27) for it is not a path of our making, but rather a path of intention...

a path intended for us, and one for which are intended.

With growing faith and dissipating fear, we can move along, go forward along the way of moving towards wholeness, away from that which divides...

a wholeness within ourselves that becomes real when lived out within community...

a community that has deepening sense of what it is trying to be and become for the larger wholes within which it looks to carry out particular work and roles...

And moving away from divisiveness, we can experience a releasing and letting go of that which unrealistically separates – that which interferes with and occludes the truth of our intended oneness...

a oneness and wholeness within ourselves, within our community, within the community of life...

a oneness and wholeness that is both an acknowledgement and a manifestation of the truth of our shared commonness – the commonness of being a people of earth, a people of a Common Source...

a people, living members of life, uniquely gifted, intended like all members of life to serve and live in accord with larger and higher – intentional – purposes.

Further reflecting on faith, we notice that ultimately faith is a manifested expression of an ongoing commitment to truth, perhaps the ultimate truth, that *through love all things are possible* (Cf. Mt 19:26; 1Jn 4:8)...

love, that which we are not the source of, but are intended to be instruments for it entering into the working of the world.

Love entering through essence makes possible this

transcending shift, this shift of moving towards wholeness, away from that which divides – of moving away from darkness and towards the light...

the shift, a real change, a movement to a uniquely and genuinely higher ground enabled by and requiring compassion, the compassion of equality, the particular manifestation of love needing to enter, to flow between and among us, at this time of potential...

an essence-to-essence flowing, the means and way for our loving one another...

a way of *being like children* (Cf. Mt 18:2) – of living from essence, of being innerly expressed, of taking on work and roles that ultimately become manifestations of our spirit, spirit that becomes available to all forever...

a way that recognizes the truth – the truth that in reality, regardless of which purposeful cycle of life we are in, we are all children...

children of a Common Father, a Common Source, nourished by a common mother, mother earth – the intended nourishing source for all of life, the whole of life, of which we are members.

Finally, what emerges from this reflection are echoes – echoes within the heart, echoes to enable our going forward at this time of potential, a time of a path of faith and dissipating fear, faith in intent and intended ways of working, faith in *through love all things are possible* (Cf. Mt 19:26; 1Jn 4:8)...

a time of love entering through essence, of essence-to-essence means for loving one another...

through the compassion of caring about, a time of moving towards wholeness and intended oneness...

and a time of *being like children* (Cf. Mt 18:2), living from essence and manifesting spirit.

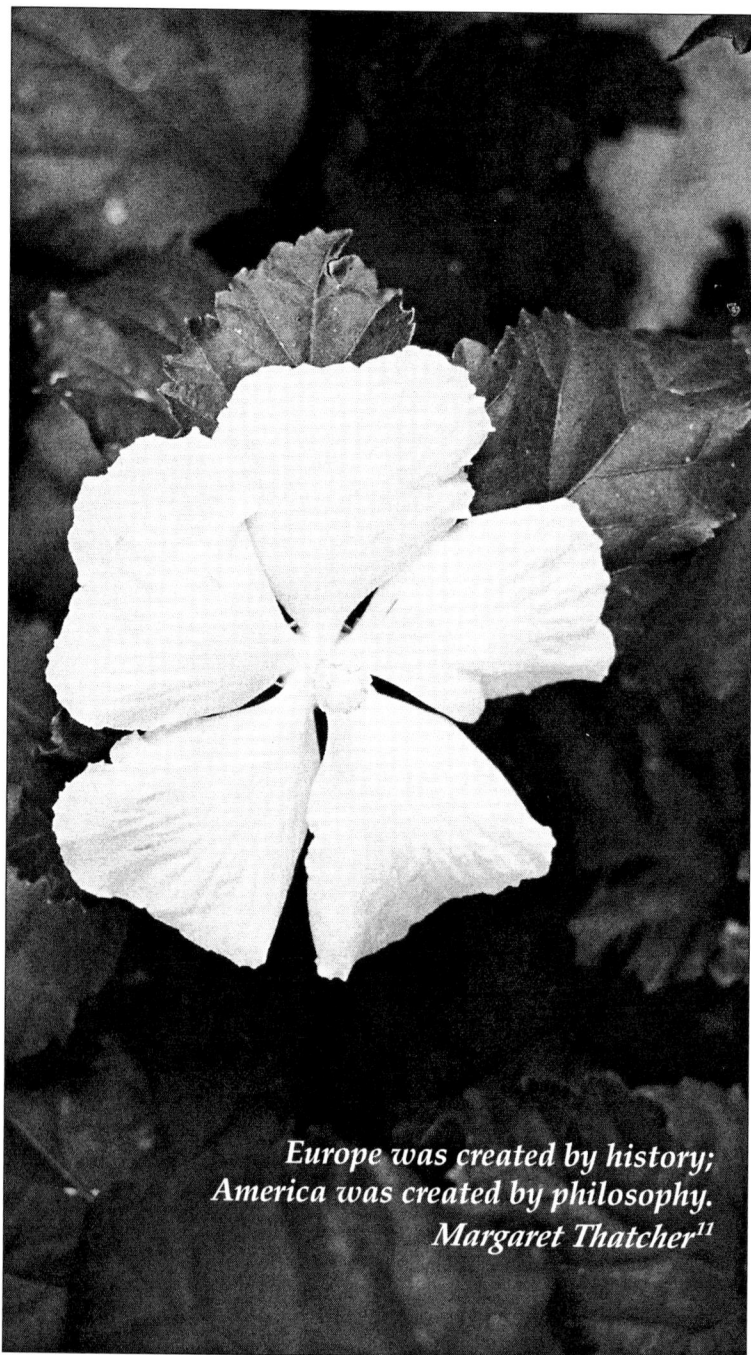

Europe was created by history;
America was created by philosophy.
                    Margaret Thatcher[11]

America's Calling

At this time of potential, there is a need for we the people to become clear about America's intended purpose in the world, her way of working, of engaging, of interacting, of leading, etc. … an intended purpose that will truly awaken the spirit of each and all of her people… a manifesting of spirit of each and all possible through the heartfelt embracing and seeing of our working philosophy, our intentional purpose, and our steadfastness towards living out our ethical principles… the essential reason for America coming into being – that which represents her true calling in the world.

As Americans, inherent within us as a people, is the capacity for *compassion*… compassion for the whole – what is good for all, for all of humanity, and all of life on earth – as well as compassion of the heart – what is right for each, for realizing the potential of each and every one of us on this earth. And as we have seen, equally imbedded within ourselves is the capacity for *courage of conscience*, courage to act from conscience – to act from and towards the good and the right.

Yet at times – perhaps at most times – we forget… we become disconnected from our heart of hearts; we lose our way, so to speak. And by so doing, we can neither bring forth, nor live out and from, these essential capacities… capacities for compassion and courage of conscience that hold within them the potential for moving us towards wholeness – towards wholeness as a people, towards peace among all people, and towards harmony with the life processes of earth… all of which by their very nature require more reflective holistic approaches, approaches that move us away from divisiveness and towards intended wholeness.

The words, *"work for all children, all children in the world,"* are a continuous awakening to our calling. These words serve not only to keep us awake to our calling, but also serve as a conscience maintainer. These words sum up our essential American philosophy of life and living... a living philosophy that continually calls us to live from the compassion of our heart, and the courage of our conscience... a living philosophy that continuously guides us to work to "see" and to unfold the open-ended potential enfolded within each, and within all.

Revitalizing our American philosophy is a process of reflection, not reaction... as such it cannot be directed, mandated, legislated or imposed... revitalizing our American philosophy of life and way of living is a grassroots process, a process of each and all. Regardless of where we are in life, or for that matter, who we are, we each have a unique purpose and calling to discover and to take up our intended role in the work for all children – all children in the world. By so doing, we move ourselves - as a person, as a people - towards becoming more fully and truly human, becoming that which all children are intended to become. Inherent within taking up a role is the joining in community with others... joining to engage in purposeful sorting out sessions, followed up with ongoing reflective work sessions, processes that enable us to see and understand the called-for work and way of working, enabling us to go forth with compassion in our processes and the courage to act from conscience.

"WORK FOR ALL CHILDREN" PURPOSEFUL SORTING OUT SESSIONS

INTENTIONAL PURPOSE OF SORTING OUT SESSIONS:

To come together and engage in a sorting out process…
> …in a way that is reflective – non-argumentative…
> …such that we can be more deliberate and wise in our choices, and pursue more fruitful paths for our children and our country.

WORKING PHILOSOPHY OF SORTING OUT SESSIONS:

There are times in our own lives when we recognize the need to step aside from our daily busyness, from what is becoming too complicated to manage – to pause, to reflect upon what is real, what is necessary, what is energizing, what is draining and therefore burdensome… a reflective pause aimed at sorting out, gaining some clarity of direction, a renewed sense of purpose.

There are times in the life of our country when sorting out is also necessary. Today is such a time. Sorting out the real from the unnecessary is greatly enhanced by going to essence, through seeing what is at work, and seeing the intended way of working – of things, processes and systems. Sorting out is further enhanced by seeing things more holistically and systemically – how significant elements relate one to another.

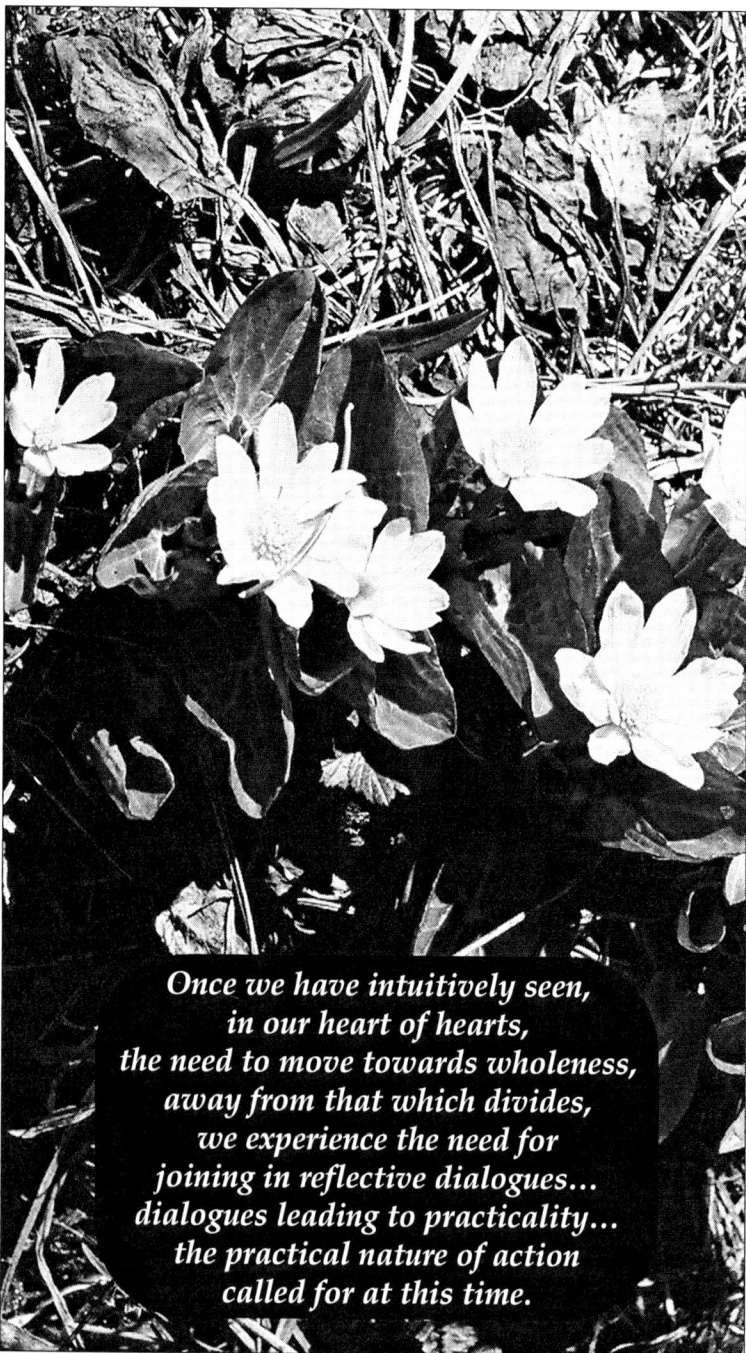

Once we have intuitively seen,
in our heart of hearts,
the need to move towards wholeness,
away from that which divides,
we experience the need for
joining in reflective dialogues...
dialogues leading to practicality...
the practical nature of action
called for at this time.

"WORK FOR ALL CHILDREN" REFLECTIVE WORK SESSIONS

WORKING PHILOSOPHY OF REFLECTIVE WORK SESSIONS:

Through love all things are possible, especially the particular... the particular to which we are each called, the particular to which we are all called, the particular for which we are supposed to stay awake – to be alert for – such that we do not miss our calling, but rather authentically respond in the manner intended.

INTENTIONAL PURPOSE OF REFLECTIVE WORK SESSIONS:

The particular particular to which we are being called at this time is...

> ...to move towards wholeness, away from that which divides...
> ...and to do so in a way that works for all children, all children in the world...
> ...such that we make a real advancement in our humanness – advancing to become a true human community, a living whole... as opposed to a loose collection of fragmented parts... an intentionally working community that enriches life... the life of the whole, and the whole of life on this earth.

"WORK FOR ALL CHILDREN" PROCESSES:

All "work for all children" processes share the common aim of moving towards wholeness - away from that which divides... wholeness for ourselves as a people of earth, a people who share a Common Source.

Moving towards wholeness is a reflective, intuitive process. As such we use these ethical principles to guide and enable our processing:

ETHICAL PRINCIPLES OF REFLECTIVE WORK SESSIONS:

- Seek to be reflective and to support the process of reflecting.

- Work towards building images, to "see"... and then understand.

- Be receptive to heartfelt direction and roles.

- Strive to be okay with "living in the question" – the experience of the process of enabling intended unfolding – versus satisfying the need for "concrete/final" answers.

- Seek to "see" what love looks like if it is to be present, actively present, in our chosen direction and roles.

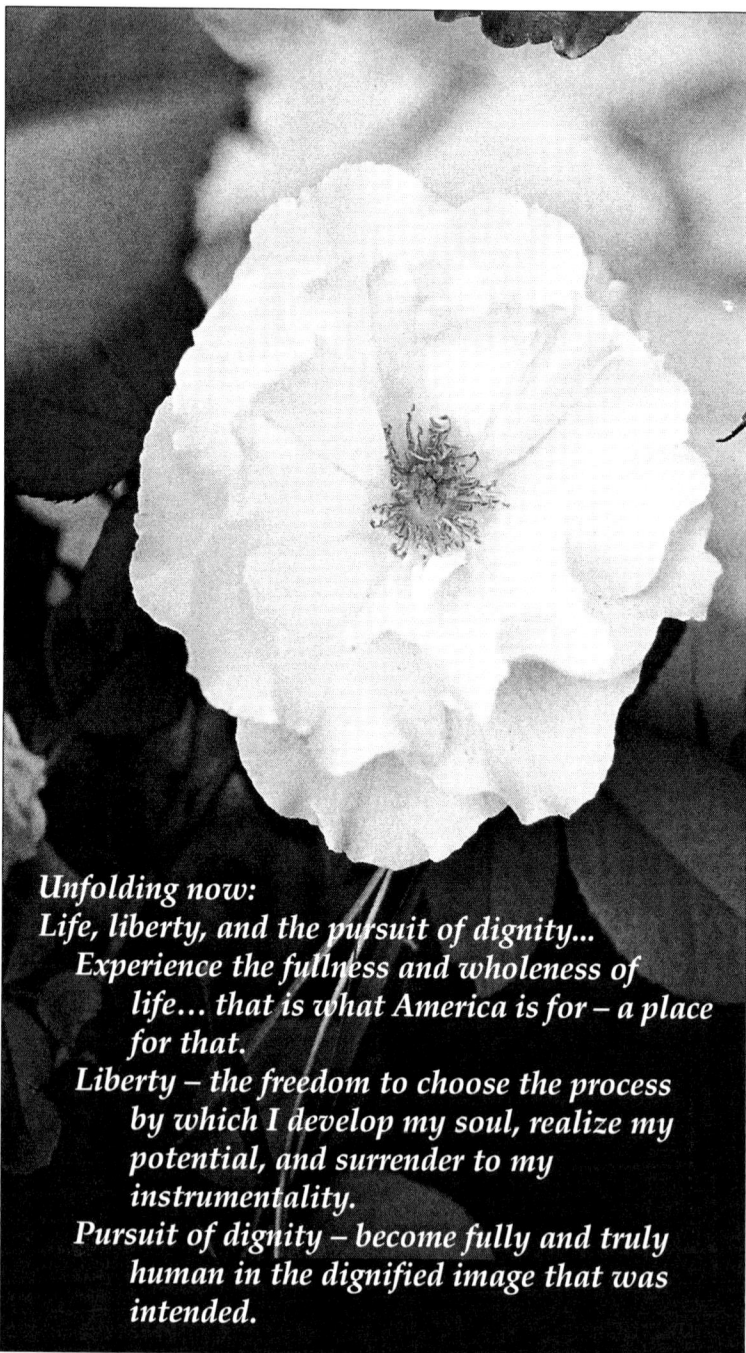

Unfolding now:
Life, liberty, and the pursuit of dignity...
   Experience the fullness and wholeness of
      life... that is what America is for – a place
      for that.
   Liberty – the freedom to choose the process
      by which I develop my soul, realize my
      potential, and surrender to my
      instrumentality.
   Pursuit of dignity – become fully and truly
      human in the dignified image that was
      intended.

The Going Forward Path
-Revitalizing America's Philosophy

This work – the work of developing philosophy, purpose and ethics –, the called-for work at this time of potential, is not foreign to us, the people of America. America was intentionally created by philosophy… a philosophy that reflected the intent of her creators… one grounded in the acknowledgement of a Source greater than ourselves, an endowing Source… a philosophy that uniquely established that the power of governance would be sourced in, reside within, the people themselves… a philosophy that firmly planted within the intended way of working of our country, the nourishing seed of inclusivity – of openness to all… an inclusivity that has been and continues to be a source of ongoing hope, not only for ourselves, but for the people of the world as well… a hope that is itself nourished by a sustained connectivity to a Greater Source.

Yes, what is presently being called for is not foreign to us, yet what is asked of us is a shift – a real step beyond what we have known. It is not, however, a shift away from the path of our birth, but rather a shift that is a deeper expression of the essential truths actively present in the creation of our country… a shift that does not deny a Source greater than ourselves… a shift that at the very least requires acknowledging that we are not the source… an acknowledgement that neither requires a religious orientation, nor is exclusive to a particular religion, but a necessary acknowledgement nonetheless… a shift that requires we come together, not so much to argue, nor seek to sustain or gain advantage for one's position, but rather to reflectively develop a clear sense of purpose for that which is essential to our well being – to the well being of our children.

...A shift that emanates from what is at this time the most inclusive of perspectives: a life of the whole perspective... a perspective that includes the people of America, the people of the world... America's children, all children of the world... the whole of life on earth... a perspective and path that we, with thoughtful consideration of the two questions – *Does it work for all children, all children of the world?* and *Does it advance our humanness?* – can authentically walk upon... a path of our choosing, a path not of our making, but a path we are intended to walk upon... a path that remains open to us, and one we can remain open to, through the presence of love in the process. Thus the necessity for our being vigilant and diligent in regards to ensuring that as we go forward, *love is present in the process.*

At this time of potential,
we are called to take
a path of love in action,
a path illuminated by
a living philosophy of potential.

The Path of Love in Action

At this time of potential, we are called to take the path of love in action...

The path of intent, the path of our potential, the path of here and now, the unfolding now...

the called-for advance in our humanness, of our moving towards wholeness – away from that which divides...

a way of moving towards fulfilling the intent, the unfolding intent of the Source – towards being and becoming fully and truly human.

A path illuminated by a philosophy...

A living philosophy, a practice-able philosophy... a living philosophy whole enough to encompass the whole of life, our work and role within and through life...

a philosophy oriented towards being and becoming, anchored in essence, acknowledging the truth of our being intentional members in the community of life...

and too, honoring the presence of and seeking to understand the working of our essential, experience-able urges: our longing to return and our yearning to become.

A path of the here and unfolding now, naturally entwined with the path of our return, of the hereafter, of salvation...

An intended entwining, which requires work – intentional effort on our part...

work requiring a living philosophy whole enough, real enough, inclusive enough to enable all who are drawn to the work of advancing our humanness in ways that realistically, holistically and truly address the critical issues currently facing humankind and all life, life's processes on earth...

a way of working, a way of reflecting and reflective dialoguing, of coming together to access wisdom...

the wisdom of intuition – not so much an aim of being wise, but rather one of gaining appropriate and necessary wisdom – the wisdom of understanding intended working...

an understanding that brings voice to intuition, courage to conscience, a seeing of a way forward, forward towards intended ways of living and working.

A path of intent...

Intent which precedes, came before, the word and the works – the whole of creation, the unfolding creation, of which we are a part... not the reason for, but an essential significant element, an intended instrument...

a path of oneness and wholeness, a potential oneness and wholeness made possible by a Common Source of intent, common to the word, to the unfolding creation, and to all living beings – to each and all of humanity.

A timely path, an essential path, at this time of potential....

A path, along which there is an awakening, a stirring, a calling within and among more and more of us to move towards wholeness – away from that which divides... a time of transcending that which separates – creates divisions and divisiveness within and among us as human beings, as well as that which separates us from life, life of the whole, the whole of life and its intended ways of working...

a time of moving towards wholeness, a potential
realizable only through love, through the intentional and authentic acceptance of the truth that
if love is not present in the process, love will not
be present in the outcome...

a time of diminishing apology for our only being
human, rather one of increasing effort towards
becoming fully and truly human...

a time of going to essence, of taking on a life of the
whole perspective...

a time of seeing and understanding through essence
what love being present in the process looks
like in the revealed works - the unfolding
creation - and the revealed word, the two
primary manifestations of intent...

the intent of the Source, the Common Source, the
Source of love, truth and good... the Source
of our intended instrumentality.

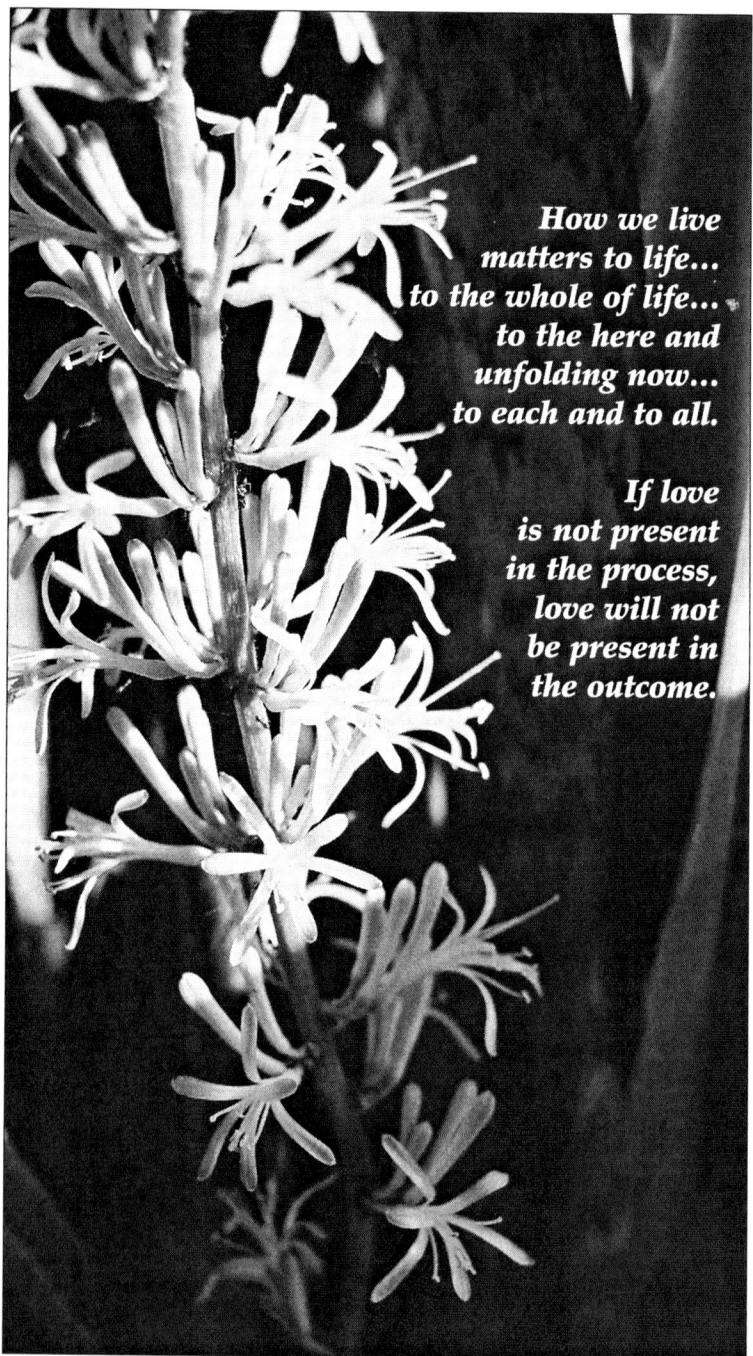

How we live
matters to life...
to the whole of life...
to the here and
unfolding now...
to each and to all.

If love
is not present
in the process,
love will not
be present in
the outcome.

"Beloved, I am writing no new commandment to you but the old commandment that you had from the beginning. The old commandment is the word that you have heard. And yet I do write a new commandment to you, which holds true in him and among you, for the darkness is passing away, and the true light is already shining. Whoever says he is in the light, yet hates his brother, is still in darkness. Whoever loves his brother remains in the light, and there is nothing in him to cause a fall" (1Jn 2:7-10).[12]

...and therein lies the hope.

NOTES

[1]*Fides et Ratio*; on the Relationship between Faith and Reason. (Boston: Pauline Books & Media, 1998), 3, 6, and Cf. 106.

[2]Anderson, Terry P., Sandra Maslow Smith, and Donna Kremer Turbyfill. Gifts of the Spirit; Experiencing Death and Loss from the Perspective of Potential. (Grand Junction: Path of Potential, 2004).

[3]Anderson, Terry P. and Sandra Maslow Smith, Who will Speak for Earth? Reflections on Securing Energy from a Life of the Whole Perspective. (Grand Junction: Path of Potential, 2006).

[4]Anderson, Terry P. and Sandra Maslow Smith, Developing Planetary Ethics; the Urgent Work of Today's Generation. (Grand Junction: Path of Potential, 2007).

[5]Anderson, Terry P., Joan Holliday, and Sandra Maslow Smith, Becoming; Right for the Heart… Good for the Whole. (Grand Junction: Path of Potential, 2005).

[6]Anderson, Terry P. and Sandra Maslow Smith, Work for All Children. (Grand Junction: Path of Potential, 2008).

[7]Cf. Pope John Paul II, *Fides et Ratio*; on the Relationship between Faith and Reason. (Boston: Pauline Books & Media, 1998), 48.

[8]"Science without religion is lame; religion without science is blind." Albert Einstein. Science, Philosophy and Religion: a Symposium, 1941.

[9]Ref. Anderson, Terry P. and Sandra Maslow Smith, Work for All Children. (Grand Junction: Path of Potential, 2008), pp. 165-173.

[10]See notes 7 & 8.

[11]British politician.

[12]The New American Bible with The Revised New Testament. (Iowa Falls, Iowa: World Bible Publishers, 1970 & 1986).